TRAVELING THE
BLUE RIDGE PARKWAY

A Guide to America's Most Scenic Drive

Craggy Pinnacle Tunnel, milepost 364

J. SCOTT GRAHAM
photographs

KERRY SCOTT JENKINS
graphic design

ELIZABETH C. HUNTER
text

and special assistance from
GARY W. JOHNSON

We would like to thank the following people for their assistance in the production of this book:

Bob Cherry, Carrie Graham, Jackie Holt, Patty Lockamy, Houck Medford, Kurt Rheinheimer, Karen Searle, Ken Thompson, Simon Thompson, & Alex White.

publishing
J. SCOTT GRAHAM
316 Shawnee Road, Johnson City, Tennessee 37604
(423) 854-9435

www.jscottgraham.com

Historical photographs and drawings courtesy of the Blue Ridge Parkway. District maps courtesy of EDAW Inc., Fort Collins, Colorado

CONTENTS

cover: View from Rough Ridge, milepost 303
left: Wild geraniums

INTRODUCTION

Landscaping, 1943, milepost 10

THERE'S A STORY THAT'S FAMOUSLY TOLD ABOUT A "WASHINGTON D.C. LADY" DRIVING THE BLUE RIDGE PARKWAY IN ITS EARLY YEARS, WHO CAME UPON A CIVILIAN CONSERVATION CORPS CREW AT WORK. THE MEN WERE TOILING IN THE RAW RED VIRGINIA CLAY, LANDSCAPING THE ROADSIDE AFTER CONSTRUCTION CREWS HAD COMPLETED THEIR WORK AND MOVED ON. EVERYTHING WAS TORN UP, PRETTY MUCH OF A MESS.

IN ALL HER HIGH DIGNITY, THE TRAVELER ALIGHTED FROM HER CAR, STRODE OVER TO THE CREW'S FOREMAN AND DEMANDED TO KNOW WHAT WAS GOING ON.

"THE BOYS ARE DOING SOME ROADSIDE STABILIZATION AND PLANTING," HE TOLD HER.

Mountain laurel, milepost 409

SHE DREW HERSELF UP. "I DON'T CARE FOR THIS," SHE SAID. "I LIKE IT MUCH BETTER BACK THERE, WHERE YOU HAVEN'T DONE ANYTHING."

The area she was referring to—where "nothing had been done"—was a section of roadside that had received, a year or two earlier, the same treatment the CCC boys were applying to the torn up mess. Unwittingly, the Washington lady had paid the highest possible compliment to the landscape architects whose artistry had produced a grand illusion: that a road could be laid down through some of the most rugged country in eastern America without disturbing anything.

Fenced haystack and worm fencing, late 1940s

THE BLUE RIDGE PARKWAY was the longest federally planned roadway in the United States when construction began in 1935. It connects two national parks—Shenandoah and Great Smoky Mountains—via a national rural parkway, the first such road to be conceived, designed and constructed as a leisure driving experience.

A Great Depression make-work project, the parkway provided thousands of unemployed men with construction jobs and used a host of New Deal programs to acquire land for and develop a chain of recreational areas that are strung along its 469 miles like beads on a string. Civilian Conservation Corps, Works Progress Administration and Emergency Relief Administration crews cleared right-of-way, landscaped roadsides and built trails, campgrounds and picnic shelters in the pre-war years.

Mabry Mill, milepost 176

Completed in 1987, the parkway remains the highest and longest continuous route in the Appalachian region. It provides scenic access to the crests and ridges of five mountain ranges, crosses six major rivers and passes through two states, 29 counties, four national forests and an Indian reservation.

As an example of pre- and post-war automotive rural parkway design, it retains the greatest degree of integrity of any parkway in the United States. Recognized as an international model of

sugar maple

landscape and engineering design achievement, it blends with its environment while it preserves and interprets cultural landscapes and historic architecture characteristic of the Central and Southern Appalachian highlands.

An uninterrupted corridor along a north/south axis, the parkway protects a diverse range of flora and fauna, including rare and endangered species, and contains areas designated as national natural landmarks. Its geologic features, varied scenery and vivid floral and fall foliage displays attract 20 million people annually, the highest visitation for any site in the National Park system.

Walnut Cove Overlook, milepost 396

Overpass construction, 1938, near Mabry Mill

USE THIS BOOK

WHAT'S A PARKWAY ANYWAY—as opposed to a highway, or ordinary two-lane road? The National Park Service's National Parkways Handbook provides a definition of a national one: "a federally owned, elongated park featuring a road designed for pleasure travel, and embracing scenic, recreational or historic features of national significance. Access from adjoining properties is limited and commercial traffic is not permitted. A national parkway has sufficient merit and character to make it a national attraction and not merely a means of travel from one region to another."

That definition provides a framework for this book. First the parkway is organized into four DISTRICTS (the same ones parkway administrators use):

1.   Ridge (Shenandoah National Park to Roanoke)
2.   Plateau (Roanoke to the Virginia/North Carolina line)
3.   Highlands (state line to Beacon Heights,
       near Grandfather Mountain)
4.   Pisgah, or Mountain (Beacon Heights to Great Smoky
       Mountains National Park)

Our only deviation from parkway nomenclature is to add "Mountain" to Pisgah (because we wanted its name to be as descriptive as those of the first three districts).

Mountain laurel through Doughton Park, milepost 242

Each district section includes a narrative description; lists highlights, elevations, visitor centers and other amenities; summarizes views and construction history; and provides thumbnail sketches of recreational areas. If your parkway travels are limited to one district, read that section first. *(But glance through the others; you may find you want to extend your trip.)*

The rest of the book covers topics that apply no matter which part you're visiting. DESIGN includes discussions of everything you'll notice as you drive, from bridges and tunnels to mileposts and signs. In FEATURES you'll find information about weather, flora and fauna, and recreational activities to engage in as you "ride awhile, stop awhile." (In this section, you'll also find our personal "Parkway Picks"— arbitrary listings of our favorite places to picnic, hike or see fall foliage.) The last section, RESOURCES, contains phone numbers and websites, parkway rules and regulations, and information about organizations that have entered into partnerships with the parkway to help it perform its mission. Sections are color-coded so you can find your way around—and cross-referenced with information here and there to point your way to items of interest. This book is designed to be user-friendly and informative—to explain some of the "whys" behind what you'll find along this amazing road. Have a great trip!

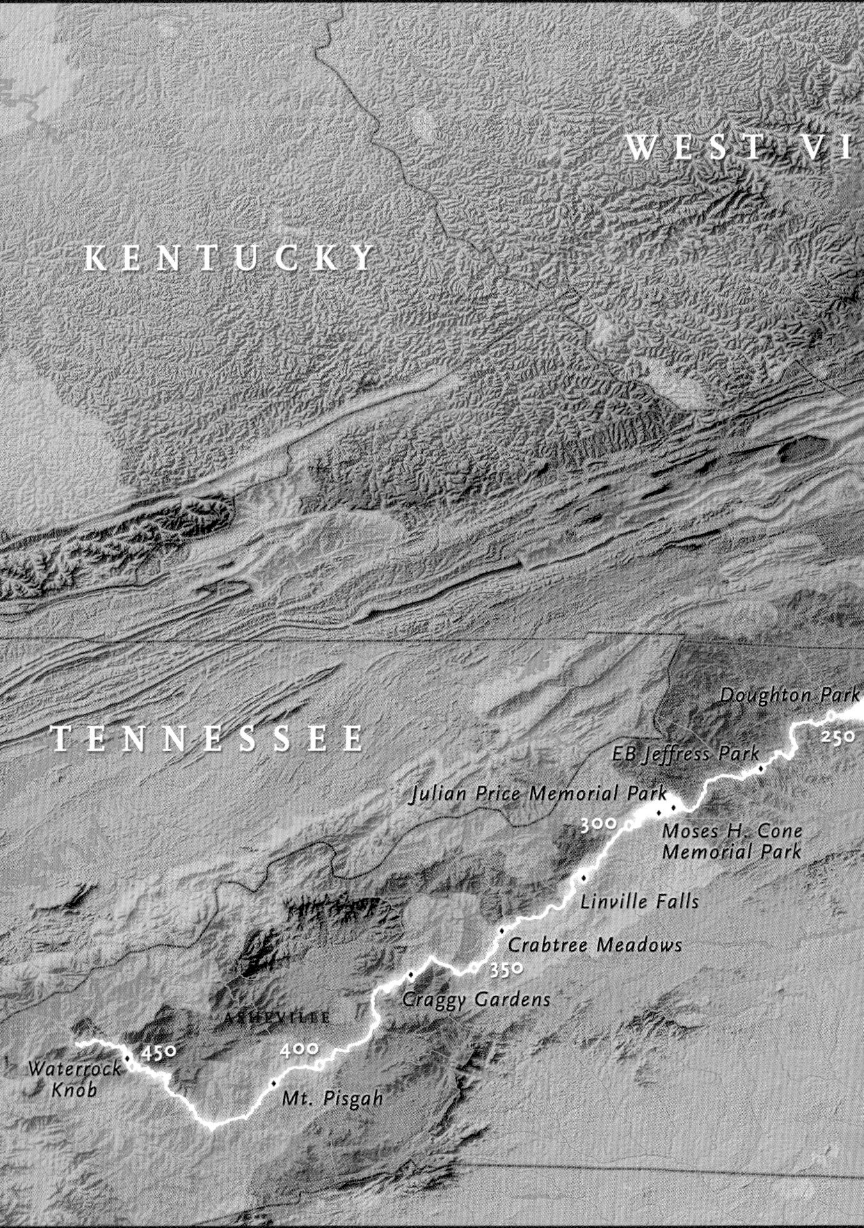

WEST VI

KENTUCKY

TENNESSEE

Doughton Park

250

EB Jeffress Park

Julian Price Memorial Park

300

Moses H. Cone
Memorial Park

Linville Falls

Crabtree Meadows

350

Craggy Gardens

ASHEVILLE

450

400

Waterrock
Knob

Mt. Pisgah

From Rockfish Gap to Roanoke...

THE

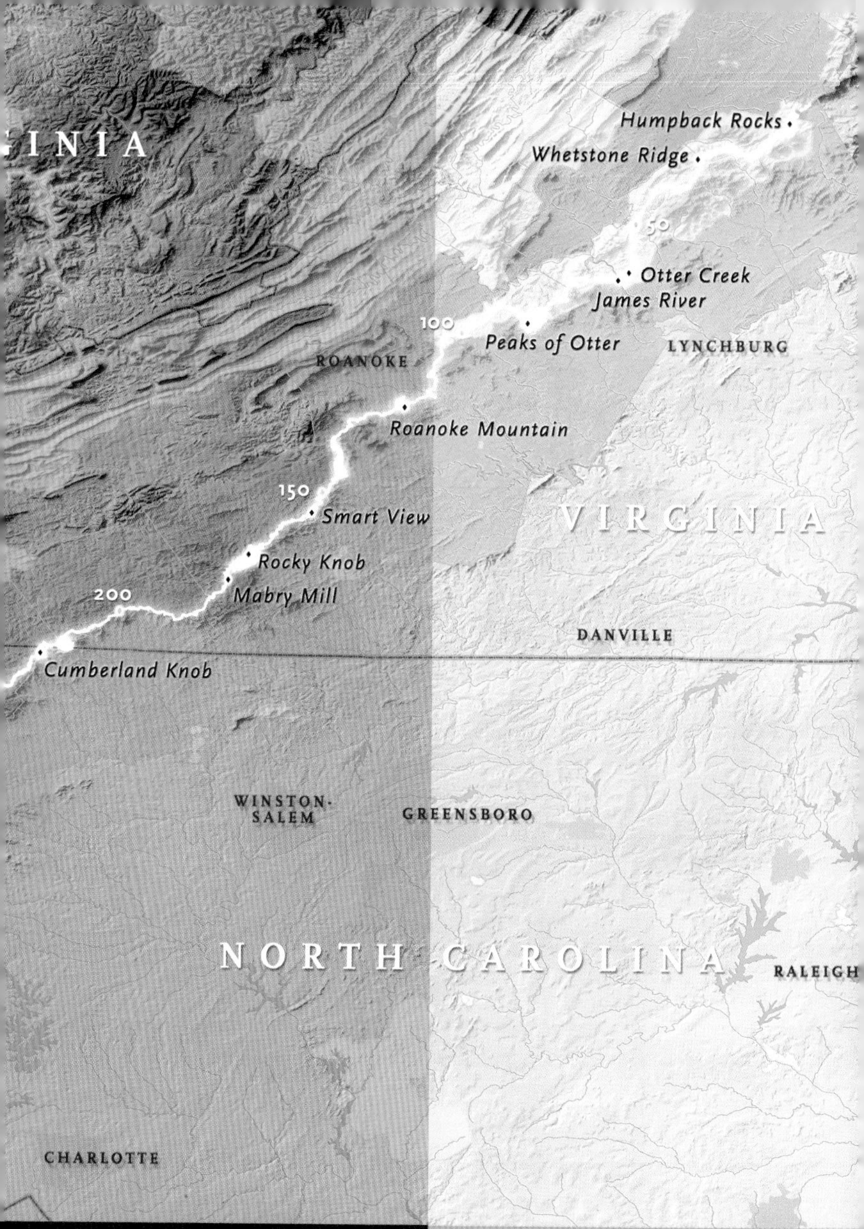
INIA
Humpback Rocks
Whetstone Ridge
50
Otter Creek
James River
100
Peaks of Otter
LYNCHBURG
ROANOKE
Roanoke Mountain
150
Smart View
VIRGINIA
Rocky Knob
200
Mabry Mill
DANVILLE
Cumberland Knob
WINSTON-SALEM
GREENSBORO
NORTH CAROLINA
RALEIGH
CHARLOTTE

MILEPOST

0–106

RIDGE

THE RIDGE: 0-106
From Rockfish Gap to Roanoke

	MILE POST
Visitor Centers	
Humpback Rocks	5.8
James River	63.6
Peaks of Otter	85.9
Campgrounds	
Otter Creek (45 tent, 24 RV)	60.9
Peaks of Otter (82 tent, 59 RV)	85.9
Picnic Areas	
Humpback Rocks	8.5
James River	63.6
Peaks of Otter	85.9
Lodging/Restaurants	
Otter Creek (restaurant only)	60.9
Peaks of Otter (open year-round)	85.6
Elevation Extremes	
High point: **3950** ft., at Apple Orchard Mountain *(high point for Virginia portion of the parkway)*	76.7
Low point: **649.4** ft., near James River *(low point for the entire parkway)*	63.0

Fallingwater Cascades, milepost 83

Humpback Rock, milepost 6

For much of the Ridge district's 106 miles, you chart a course not unlike that of the turkey vultures that ceaselessly tilt and glide above the ridgetop on sunny afternoons. It's as though you've wind beneath your wings, almost from the moment you begin the climb out of Rockfish Gap, a historically important mountain pass on a busy trade route. To the west are Waynesboro, Staunton and the Shenandoah Valley, a NE/SW-trending trough of rich farmland bounded by the Blue Ridge and Allegheny Mountains; to the east, Rockfish Valley, Charlottesville, Richmond and, far beyond the horizon, the Atlantic Ocean. Rockfish Gap remains a busy transportation corridor: I-64, US 250 and a railroad tunnel all pass beneath the place where Shenandoah National Park's Skyline Drive ends and the Blue Ridge Parkway begins.

Before you've driven your first parkway mile, the views begin to the east. The parkway rises steadily as a bird on an updraft along the slope toward the ridgetop, then tips a wing to swoop through a gap. In its first 100 miles it rises and descends this way repeatedly, offering valley views to the west and east in about equal numbers. Occasionally it follows the knife-blade crest of the Blue Ridge—the mountainside falling off sharply just beyond the shoulder on both sides of the road—for several relatively level miles. The Ridge district is the only part of the parkway where you feel this sensation.

For the first half of its journey, the road flirts from midslope to ridge and back again before losing altitude to surrender to a seven-mile infatuation with Otter Creek. It dances across the waterway nine times before the creek flows into Otter Lake, an artificial impoundment. Approaching the James River, it reaches its lowest elevation (649.4 feet). The river crossed, it remembers its love affair with the high and lonesome. In 14 miles it climbs 3200 feet to reach the summit of Apple Orchard Mountain, its Virginia high point, reverses itself to begin a 12-mile plunge toward Powell's Gap, passing through the forested valley of Peaks of Otter on the way. After another series of ups and downs, it regains the ridgetop at Harvey's Knob, follows it for several miles, then glides down slope toward the Roanoke Valley, where the Plateau District begins.

Catawba rhododendron

Driving the Ridge today is largely a forested experience, though much of the land was cleared for farmland or harvested for timber a century ago. Jefferson and Washington national forests bound the parkway 90 percent of the time. But there are short—and memorable—breaks in the woods near Love Gap (MP 15.4) and Whetstone Ridge (MP 29) where adjacent privately owned open land billows like a sail. While the district is rich in natural history, its treasures include its cultural sites: a farm museum at Humpback Rocks; canal locks at the James River; and Polly Wood's Ordinary and Johnson Farm at Peaks of Otter.

White-tailed deer

HIGHLIGHTS

Five Virginia wilderness areas—Three Ridges, the Priest, St. Mary's, James River Face and Thunder Ridge—are visible from parkway overlooks.

Several overlooks (in addition to the Ridge's recreational areas) offer glimpses into the region's past. Stone "hog fences," reputedly built by slaves, snake between Humpback Rocks and Greenstone Overlook (MP 8.8). Look them over on the 0.2-mile self-guiding trail that begins at the overlook and interprets the volcanic origins of local rock formations. At Yankee Horse Ridge (MP 34.4), find a reconstructed section of railroad track that carried more than a million board feet of lumber when virgin timber was harvested here in the early 20th century.

The parkway provides access to or crosses the Appalachian Trail 25 times in its first 100 miles. (Parking is available on the parkway or a short distance from it at most of these intersects.) Further south, motor road and footpath diverge, so if you want to hike a bit of the AT, do it here.

Virginia's only parkway tunnel—through Bluff Mountain—occurs at the Ridge district's midpoint (MP 53). The next tunnel won't occur for 280 miles.

The parkway's only on-parkway year-round lodgings and restaurant are located at Peaks of Otter (MP 85.6)

Views

This section's most memorable views are bird's eye panoramas from midslope and ridgetop perches into valleys to the east and west. Anomalies: a section between MP 24-30, with closer views of agricultural scenes in open uplands; and the James River Water Gap, where the parkway makes its most picturesque river crossing.

Construction history

The parkway was divided into 44 sections for construction purposes: 20 in Virginia and 24 in North Carolina. Before World War II halted parkway construction, many sections were being built simultaneously. Nine of the Ridge district's ten sections—a total of 97.7 miles—were finished by 1942. Its final section—from Black Horse Gap (MP 97.7) to US 460 (MP 105.8)—was constructed between 1946-50. (Note: The 1040' Harry Flood Byrd Memorial Bridge across the James River wasn't completed until 1960. Until then, travelers had to detour to cross the James.)

RECREATIONAL AREAS

HUMPBACK ROCKS/FARM MUSEUM (MP 5.8-8.8)

Humpback Rocks—a jagged outcrop one mile up a zigzagging trail crowned by spectacular views into Rockfish and Shenandoah Valleys—has long been a local landmark. But it was the "gentle sloping pasture land surrounded by fine forest on the slopes of Humpback Mountain below 'The Rocks'" that caught parkway designer Stan Abbott's eye. Plans drawn up in 1934—before the parkway had a name or construction had begun—called for a developed area in this field-and-forest mosaic. The plans included some facilities (a service station, inn and campground) that were never constructed, and picnic grounds and hiking trails that were. This is the first contact station for southbound motorists who access the parkway from Skyline Drive or Rockfish Gap. Its most popular feature is a quarter-mile wheelchair-accessible trail through a mountain farm exhibit. Though it's located

Humpback Rocks Farm Museum, milepost 6

James River from the Trail of Trees, milepost 64

on the site of a farmstead established by William J. Carter in 1867, the farm buildings aren't original to the site. They're reassembled from other locations, or are recreations of local farm structures. Among them are some ingenious contraptions—a weasel-proof chicken house and a bear-proof hog pen—as well as more traditional farm structures (a log cabin, spring house, barn and root cellar). Traces of the old Howardsville Turnpike—a major 19th century route—are visible across the parkway from the visitor center, which houses exhibits interpreting rural life.

OTTER CREEK/JAMES RIVER (MP 58-63.8)

Stan Abbott considered Otter Creek "one of the most attractive mountain streams along the parkway," perfect for development as "an elongated water feature park." Early plans for bathing facilities and a beach at Otter Lake were abandoned long before Otter Creek's coffee shop and campground opened in 1962. Otter Creek offers an up-close-and-personal look at a

mountain stream, with overlooks that provide access
to 3.5-mile Otter Creek Trail. This mostly-level creek-
side stroll connects to a 0.9-mile loop around Otter
Lake and continues on to the James River. The day-use
area on the banks of the James has riverside picnic
tables, a visitor center and access to a restored lock on
what was once the James River and Kanawha Canal.
The canal, in use between 1835-80, was supplanted
by the railroad that threads its way through the
James River Water Gap. The canal's builders had lofty
dreams of connecting Virginia Tidewater country
to the Ohio River. But only part of the canal, from
Richmond to Buchanan, just west of the Blue Ridge,
was ever constructed. This 195.6 mile section—with
its 98 locks, 23 dams, 12 aqueducts, 31 bridges and
199 culverts—cost more than $8 million to build.
Restored Battery Creek lock, constructed in 1848,
is accessible via a pedestrian walkway suspended
beneath the parkway bridge. The 0.4-mile trail to the
lock is one of two beginning below the visitor center.

Abbott Lake at Peaks of Otter, milepost 86

The other, a 0.4-mile self-guiding "Trail of Trees,"
winds up the river bluff and through the forest. Its
trailhead is just before the footbridge.

PEAKS OF OTTER (MP 83.1-85.9)

"We need artificial lakes in national parks about
as much as I need bloomers," spluttered former
National Park Service director George Hartzog Jr.,
when he learned of plans for one at Peaks of Otter.
But Hartzog's disdain didn't keep Abbott Lake from
being built at the parkway's most popular Virginia
recreational area. The lake's waters reflect Sharp Top
—one of the three peaks for which the area is named.
In 1939, when the pleasure road penetrated the valley
beneath the peaks, it entered a community long used
to catering to travelers. In pre-Civil War days, you
could put up for the night at Polly Wood's Ordinary,

a small hostelry that once stood on ground that Abbott Lake flooded. (The Ordinary was one of two log structures whose sites the lake inundated. Historians disagree as to whether the right one was preserved.) More spacious guest accommodations were soon available at Otter Peaks Hotel, which opened in 1857 and burned to the ground 13 years later. The Hotel Mons replaced it and hosted travelers until 1936. Most of the two dozen families who lived in the Peaks area farmed, but they also earned cash money from the tourist trade. Part of the 4100 acres the recreational area includes was purchased from private landowners, but the US Forest Service transferred ownership of more than 3400 acres to the park service in 1941. A 19th century toll road took sightseers to Sharp

Top's summit; the Civilian Conservation Corps built the current road up Sharp Top. CCC boys also erected a fire tower (dismantled after WWII) on the mountaintop. Abbott Lake, dammed and flooded in 1964, eliminated a chronically marshy area and created a quiet spot for anglers to cast a line. The recreation area has seven trails. Two of them—the Flat Top and Fallingwater Cascades trails—were jointly designated a National Recreational Trail in 1982. Another leads to the Johnson Farm, an isolated farmstead restored to interpret mountain life in the 1930s. The house is open May through October, but you can explore the log barn and outbuildings or peek in windows any time of year.

spring beauty

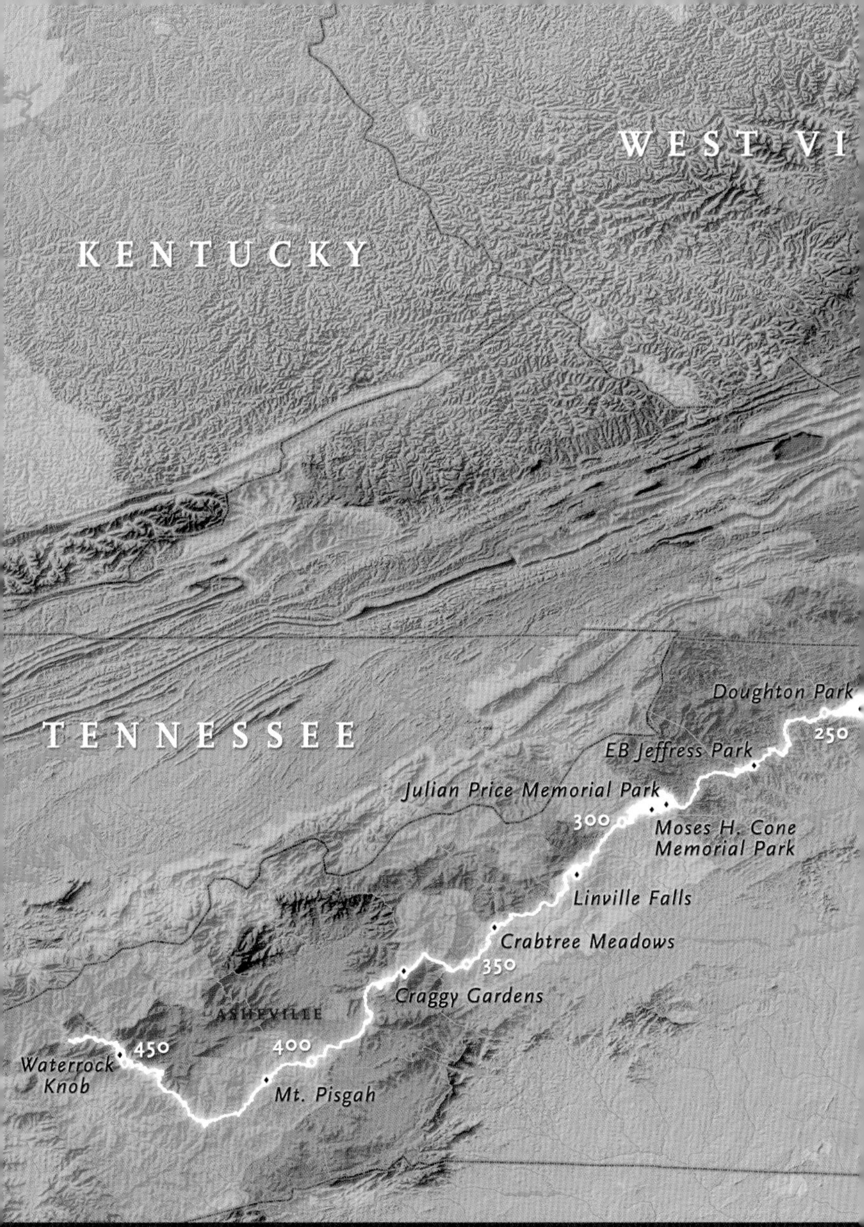

WEST VI

KENTUCKY

TENNESSEE

Doughton Park

250

EB Jeffress Park

Julian Price Memorial Park

300

Moses H. Cone
Memorial Park

Linville Falls

Crabtree Meadows

350

Craggy Gardens

ASHEVILLE

450

400

Waterrock
Knob

Mt. Pisgah

From Roanoke to VA/NC State Line…

THE PL

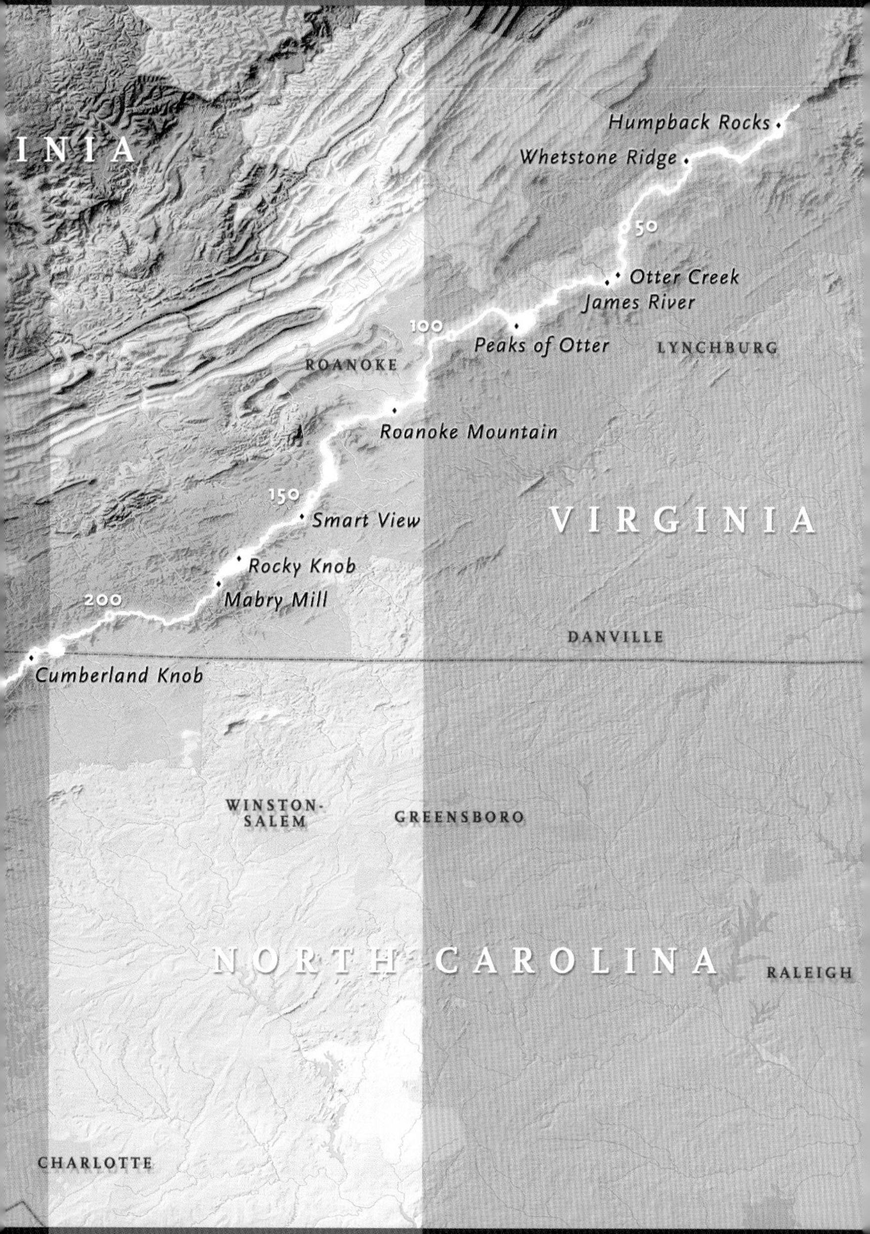
INIA
Humpback Rocks
Whetstone Ridge
50
Otter Creek
James River
100
Peaks of Otter
LYNCHBURG
ROANOKE
Roanoke Mountain
150
Smart View
VIRGINIA
Rocky Knob
200
Mabry Mill
DANVILLE
Cumberland Knob
WINSTON-SALEM
GREENSBORO
NORTH CAROLINA
RALEIGH
CHARLOTTE

MILEPOST

106–217

ATEAU

THE PLATEAU: 106-217

From Roanoke to VA/NC State Line

Visitor Centers

	MILE POST
Blue Ridge Parkway Visitor Center at Virginia's Explore Park	115.0
Rocky Knob	169.0

Campgrounds

Roanoke Mountain (74 tent, 30 RV)	120.4
Rocky Knob (81 tent, 28 RV)	167.1

Picnic Areas

Smart View	154.5
Rocky Knob	169.0
Groundhog Mountain	188.8

Lodging/Restaurants

Rocky Knob Housekeeping Cabins (lodgings only) *(cabins are on VA 758/Woodberry Road, one mile off parkway)*	174.1
Mabry Mill (restaurant only)	176.2

Elevation Extremes

High point: **3471** ft., where parkway crosses VA 726 near Rocky Knob. The parkway through Rocky Knob Recreational Area remains above 3000', dropping below 3000' at Belcher Curve, MP 172.7 *(no sign, but this sweeping curve, with its post-and-rail fencing, is a distinctive parkway landmark)*	171.7
Low point: **965** ft., crossing Roanoke River	114.9

Puckett Cabin, milepost 190

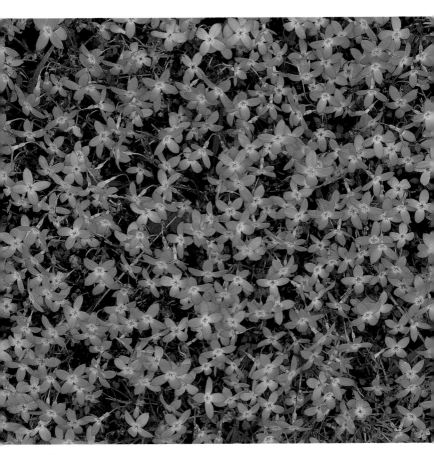

Bluets

Nowhere is the change from one parkway district to another more distinct than the switch from Ridge to Plateau. The whole character of the land changes, from a "crest of the Blue Ridge" experience to immersion in an agricultural landscape of pastures and hayfields, cattle and cabbages. It was Plateau Country that inspired designer Stan Abbott to describe the parkway as "a museum of the American countryside."

The change isn't apparent immediately. The parkway must first traverse the Roanoke Valley before ascending to Adney Gap (MP 136), one of its most beautiful and unspoiled agricultural landscapes. More of the same follows, as the road swings in generous arcs, in gentle dips and rises, through farmland interspersed with patches of forest. This pattern continues past Smart View and Rakes Millpond (MP 162.4) until the road approaches Rocky Knob, Plateau

Country's dramatic high point. Here it skirts highland pastures and skims the rim of forested Rock Castle Gorge. It descends through long, sweeping Belcher Curve (MP 172.7) to re-enter a patchwork of woods and rolling open country. It soon passes some of its most famous roadside cultural landmarks: Mabry Mill, Groundhog Mountain and Puckett Cabin. Like a boat breasting a series of ocean swells, it rises and falls through Volunteer, Orchard and Fancy gaps, where the modern day fate of once picturesque farmland is all too apparent.

Plateau Country views are more vulnerable than those in any other district. Its open nature makes it difficult—sometimes impossible—to screen the parkway from encroaching residential development in the Roanoke Valley and changing land use patterns elsewhere. Still, parkway agricultural leases and scenic easements (see p. 85 in Design) succeed, as Stan Abbott hoped they would, in bringing the rural farm scene "up to the fence at the edge of the road."

Dogwood along Orchard Gap, milepost 194

Highlights

The parkway's most recent road construction project—the Roanoke River Parkway, a 1.5-mile spur road to Virginia's Explore Park—occurs at MP 115. Overlooks along this spur road offer views of undeveloped countryside in the Roanoke Valley. Explore Park is a recreation park and outdoor living history museum developed through a partnership between the parkway, Explore Park and Roanoke County.

Cahas Knob Parking Overlook (MP 139) marks the spot where the Blue Ridge Parkway and the Eastern Continental Divide begin to closely coincide. From this point south—until the parkway and the Blue Ridge diverge near Mt. Mitchell (MP 355.3)—streams east of the parkway flow into the Atlantic Ocean, while those to its west eventually empty into the Gulf of Mexico.

Rural sights worth noting in Plateau Country include Kelley Schoolhouse (on Schoolhouse Road, at MP 149.1) and numerous church and family cemeteries. One of three stone churches—Bluemont Presbyterian Church (MP 191.9)—is visible from the roadway. You'll have to detour slightly to see the others: Slate Mountain Presbyterian Church (turn at MP 174.1 onto VA 758/Woodberry Road—the road to Rocky Knob Housekeeping Cabins—then left onto Rock Church Road); Mayberry Presbyterian Church (turn at MP 180.1 onto VA 600. Church is a few hundred feet from parkway and Mayberry Country Store).

There are more than 100 at-grade crossings of public and private roads in Plateau country, more than in any other parkway district. (Be aware that farm and other vehicles may cross the parkway in front of you.)

Views

Predominant views—pastoral scenes of rural farms and agriculture—are up close and intimate in Plateau Country, where you drive through (rather than look down on) "the scenery." This district illustrates what

Stan Abbott meant when he described the parkway as a "park without boundaries." Though the parkway's boundary line is almost always within view—and though most adjacent land is privately owned—it's hard to tell where one ends and the other begins.

Yellow-bellied slider turtles

CONSTRUCTION HISTORY

The first section to open to traffic in either Virginia or North Carolina is in Plateau Country: the 8.3-mile section from Adney Gap to Pine Spur Gap (MP 135.9-144.2), which opened on Dec. 19, 1936. By the end of 1939, travelers could drive 81 of the Plateau's 111 miles—from Adney Gap to the VA/NC state line—and continue another 60 miles through North Carolina's Highlands. This 141-mile section was the longest continuous parkway stretch open before World War II. Parkway construction through the Roanoke Valley languished until well after the war. A 14.7 mile section from US 220 to Adney Gap opened in 1960; five years later, the Plateau's final 15.3 miles—from US 460 to US 220—was completed.

Recreational Areas

Smart View (MP 154.5)

Smart View, a day-use area with an old log cabin, wooden fences, rustic comfort stations and picnic shelter, was one of the parkway's five original recreation areas. Its name refers to its "right smart view" of the Virginia piedmont. Resettlement Administration funds purchased its 500+ acres in 1937; development began in 1938. Emergency Relief Administration workers had completed most of the work on its picnic area by the time Smart View opened in 1940. Civilian Public Service workers (conscientious objectors) added a 2.6-mile trail that winds through its woodlands and meadows during World War II. Parkway designer Stan Abbott considered Smart View "one of the more attractive areas adjacent to the parkway, typical of the escarpment country south of Roanoke."

Northern red oak leaf

Rocky Knob (MP 167-174)

Another of the parkway's five original parks, Rocky Knob owes its size to the foresight and vision of Sam Weems, who succeeded Stan Abbott as the parkway's second superintendent. Original plans for Rocky Knob called for acquisition of only 500-600 acres; Weems, then a Resettlement Administration land appraiser, gazed into Rock Castle Gorge and recognized a gem. His superiors eventually agreed. Weems purchased nearly 3600 acres, to make Rocky Knob the parkway's largest developed area in Virginia south of Roanoke. The parkway's first building—rustic Rocky Knob trail shelter—was completed in 1937 and is worth the 0.2-mile climb to see (hike south from the Saddle overlook at MP 168). The shelter is located on 10.8-mile Rock Castle Gorge loop trail, designated a National Recreational Trail in 1984. The trail follows the rim, then drops to the base of the gorge, 2000 feet below, passing the remains of a once-thriving community (vacated for the most part before the parkway acquired gorge lands), then climbs back out. Two other items of interest: a now-mature chestnut orchard (located on a knoll in the camping area) planted in 1940 to supply farmers with a source of seed for Chinese chestnuts to replace American chestnuts destroyed by blight; and Rocky Knob's "rough-it" (housekeeping) cabins (see Lodging listing, p. 33, for directions), a prototype for other such accommodations that were planned, but never built, elsewhere on the parkway.

Mabry Mill/Groundhog Mountain/ Puckett Cabin (MP 176.2, 188.8, and 189.9)

We have grouped these three sites together because of their close proximity and the insights they offer into the region's cultural history.

Mabry Mill was built by Ed Mabry in the early 20th century, and operated by him and his "good helpmeet" Lizzie Dehart Mabry until his death in 1936. Mabry overcame serious site limitations (not enough slope nor sufficient water) to operate his mill, which he used for three purposes: to grind cornmeal, saw

logs into boards, and power a woodworking shop. A
blacksmith and wagon-maker, Ed was remembered by
neighbors as a hard worker who nonetheless relished
and always had time for a good joke or story. By the
time parkway designer Stan Abbott discovered and fell
in love with the mill, Mabry had suffered a crippling
disease and his mill had fallen into disrepair. It was
nearly destroyed by a state highway crew clearing
parkway right-of-way, who didn't know about Abbott's
plans to restore it. In 1942, the parkway restored the
mill and razed the two-story white clapboard house
that Mabry had built with lumber he sawed in his mill
and painted with a brush fashioned from a horse's
tail. The log cabin that stands in its place comes from

Mabry Mill, milepost 176

Carroll County, was reconstructed on the site in 1956-57, and has no historical relevance to the mill or the Mabrys. Nor do other mountain industry exhibits—a cane mill, sorghum press, moonshine still and other artifacts—on the loop behind the mill. Mabry's smithy was moved near the mill from elsewhere on the property to facilitate interpretation.

Groundhog Mountain was developed as a small day-use area. Civilian Public Service workers erected rail fences around its picnic area in 1939; the Virginia State Forest Service added the saddle-notched log fire lookout in 1942. Much of the original fencing has been replaced by sections of buck, picket and post-and-rail fence that illustrate fencing styles in use in the region in the 1930s.

Puckett Cabin may or may not have been the home of Orelena Puckett, a midwife who successfully delivered more than 1000 babies between 1890 and 1939, when she died at age 102. Mrs. Puckett charged $6 for her services when times were good; as little as $1 when they weren't. In winter, she hammered nails through her shoe soles to maintain purchase on icy footpaths. Her most reliable medications: soap and water and an occasional dose of whiskey laced with camphor. The cabin, built around 1865, was probably moved to the site by Mrs. Puckett's husband John for her sister-in-law's use. Orelena (her name appears variously, as Orleana and Arlene) and John most likely lived in a larger house nearby.

BLUE RIDGE MUSIC CENTER (MP 213.3)

The parkway's newest recreational area is 12 miles east of Galax, VA, a mecca for traditional Blue Ridge string band music. Galax hosts an annual fiddler's convention that draws thousands of musicians—and many more thousands of fans—each August. The convention, which began in 1935 as a local Moose lodge fundraiser, may be the oldest and is undoubtedly the largest of dozens of such events held in the mountains. The parkway's new music center is located below Fisher's Peak, the highest mountain on the VA/NC state line. The center documents and interprets traditional music of the Southern Appalachians and Blue Ridge—music that takes a multitude of forms: ballads, sacred music, work songs, blues, instrumentals, popular songs and string band music. A cooperative venture between the parkway and the National Council for the Traditional Arts, the center hosts summer weekend concerts in an outdoor amphitheatre. It also includes indoor exhibits, hiking trails and an outdoor informal music area where musicians and would-be musicians can interact.

Groundhog Mountain, milepost 189

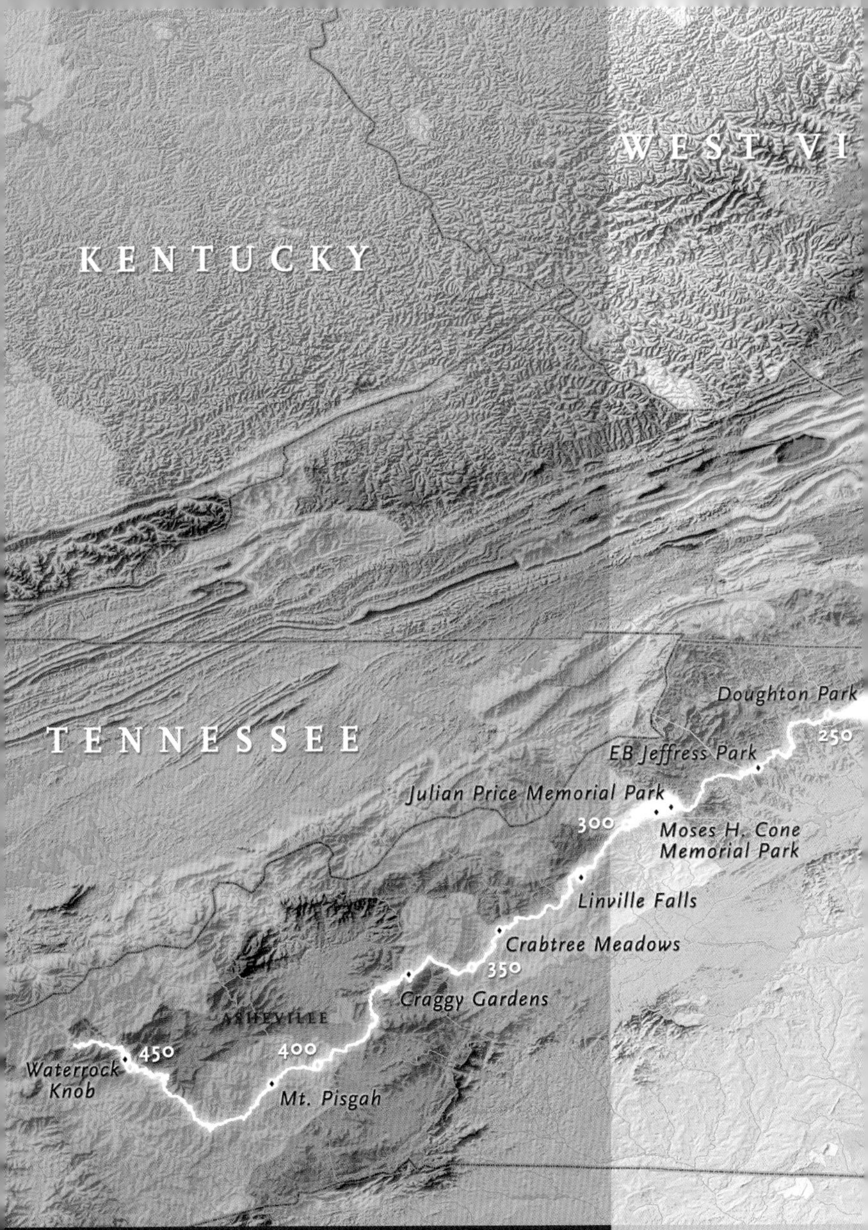

KENTUCKY

WEST VI

TENNESSEE

Doughton Park

EB Jeffress Park

Julian Price Memorial Park

250

300

Moses H. Cone
Memorial Park

Linville Falls

Crabtree Meadows

350

Craggy Gardens

ASHEVILLE

450

400

Waterrock
Knob

Mt. Pisgah

From VA/NC State Line

MILEPOS

217-30

THE HIG

Humpback Rocks

Whetstone Ridge

50

Otter Creek

James River

100

Peaks of Otter

LYNCHBURG

ROANOKE

Roanoke Mountain

VIRGINIA

150

Smart View

Rocky Knob

Mabry Mill

200

DANVILLE

Cumberland Knob

INIA

WINSTON-
SALEM

GREENSBORO

NORTH CAROLINA

RALEIGH

CHARLOTTE

to Beacon Heights...

HLANDS

5

THE HIGHLANDS: 217-305
From VA/NC State Line to Beacon Heights

	MILE POST
Visitor Centers	
Cumberland Knob	217.5
Doughton Park	241.1
Cone Manor	294.0
Linn Cove	304.4
Campgrounds	
Doughton Park (110 tent, 25 RV)	239.2
Price Park (129 tent, 68 RV)	269.9
Picnic Areas	
Cumberland Knob	217.5
Doughton Park	241.1
E.B. Jeffress Park	271.9
Price Park	296.4
Lodging/Restaurants	
Doughton Park	241.1
Elevation Extremes	
High point: **4412** ft., Yonahlossee Overlook Other high points: 3702' at concession area in Doughton Park, MP 241; 3712' at Aho Gap, MP 288; 3982' at Moses Cone Memorial Park, MP 294; and 4400' at Pilot Ridge overlook, MP 301.8.	303.9
Low point: **2555** ft., at Virginia/NC state line	217.0

Coneflowers along parkway

sunrise near Stack Rock, milepost 305

The Highlands begins at its low point—where the parkway crosses the state line—and ends near its highest. After a quiet meander along woodland creeks and past millponds whose calm surfaces reflect the sky, the road begins a gradual ascent through Doughton Park. A series of overlooks offer panoramic views: to the east, Stone Mountain's streaked and barren flanks draw the eye; to the west lay fertile valleys of Ashe and Alleghany counties. The overlooks' names are as evocative as the scenery is sumptuous: Mahoghany Rock. Devil's Garden. Air Bellows Gap.

Beyond Doughton Park's airy upland pastures and scaly Alligator Back, the parkway settles into an alternating pattern of woodlands and fields. Wild turkeys haunt grassy shoulders; tall pines cast somber shadows. For much of the way, the roadway is enclosed in forest, though here and there "windows" are thrown open to offer brief glimpses of distant blue mountains. Unchinked log cabins appear in isolated roadside glades.

Approaching Boone and Blowing Rock, the rolling countryside becomes grassier, more open, with long views mostly to the east. It is prelude to the sedate pastures and managed woodlands of the Cone Estate, summer retreat a century ago to North Carolina's "Denim King." Beyond Price Lake's placid waters, the Highlands prepares for its grand finale. The parkway takes the middle road between the rocky ramparts of Grandfather Mountain and the wilderness of Wilson's Creek. But this stunning mountainside traverse offers one grand panorama after another as it crosses its own version of China's Great Wall (MP 303) and snakes across the Linn Cove Viaduct. The Highlands yields shortly thereafter to Pisgah—the parkway's final district—at Beacon Heights.

Rosebay rhododendron

Highlights

One of the best "balcony" views of the North Carolina piedmont awaits you at the end of a 0.2-mile stroll at Fox Hunter's Paradise overlook (MP 218.4). On a clear day you can see, if not forever, as far as Winston-Salem.

Low, dry-laid stone guardwalls give a unique look to the parkway between MP 217-245.

Residents of 11 northwestern North Carolina counties craft the folk toys, musical instruments, baskets, brooms and quilts sold at Northwest Trading Post (MP 258). In search of a literal "taste of the mountains?"

Groundhog

Check out the pecan tarts, stack cakes, ham biscuits, cheese and other treats.

The exploits of two men—one famous, one infamous—are recalled at a pair of Highlands overlooks. At The Lump (MP 264.4), an interpretive sign tells the story of Tom Dula, hanged in 1868 for the murder of his sweetheart. At Boone's Trace (MP 285.1), the parkway crosses paths with legendary frontiersman Daniel Boone.

The Tanawha (Cherokee for "fabulous hawk or eagle") Trail roughly parallels the parkway between Price Lake and Beacon Heights. The 13.5-mile trail provides pedestrian access to view the Linn Cove Viaduct. Overlooks between MP 299.2-305.2 provide trail access.

VIEWS

What is most remarkable about Highlands' views is their variety. No one type of view predominates here. One moment, you're immersed in a rural valley scene; the next, you're high on a ridgetop, taking in panoramic views of forests and farmland. This sequence repeats itself again and again in the Highlands. You never have time to get tired of a particular kind of view. The ever-changing landscape invites anticipation. What's next?

CONSTRUCTION HISTORY

Both the opening and closing chapters of parkway construction history occurred in the Highlands. Construction began near Cumberland Knob on Sept. 11, 1935. Two years later, North Carolina's first completed section—Air Bellows Gap (MP 237.1) to NC 18 (MP 248)—opened to traffic. By the fall of 1939, nearly 60 continuous miles—from the Virginia state line to Deep Gap (MP 276.4)—were completed. Two of the Highlands' remaining three sections—from Deep Gap to Holloway Mountain Road (MP 298.6)— didn't open until 1960. It took another 27 years before the final 7.7-mile "Missing Link"—Holloway

Mountain Road to Beacon Heights (MP 305.2)—was completed. Fifty-two years to the day after parkway construction began, travelers could, for the first time, drive from Rockfish Gap to the Oconaluftee River without a detour.

RECREATIONAL AREAS

Flame azalea near Cumberland Knob, milepost 218

CUMBERLAND KNOB (MP 217.5)

"The first thing we did was run the sheep off," remembered one of the 100 men who gathered on Pack Murphy's farm to begin construction of the Blue Ridge Parkway on Sept. 11, 1935. He recalled that day 50 years later, when the parkway celebrated its Golden Anniversary at nearby Cumberland Knob. The first of the parkway's recreational areas to be completed, Cumberland Knob is just south of the VA/NC state line. It's "a fine vantage point overlooking the Piedmont country of North Carolina," parkway designer Stan Abbot said. The day-use area's 800 acres include two hiking trails, one leading to a chestnut and rock trail shelter built by Works Progress Administration crews. Its visitor center is housed in what was once a combination picnic shelter, sandwich shop and comfort station. Completed in 1942, it was the first parkway facility to be operated by a concessioner.

DOUGHTON PARK (MP 238.5-244.8)

With its high pastures, miles of post-and-rail fencing, rocky outcrops and dramatic views, 5410-acre Doughton Park is the largest parkway recreation area in North Carolina. Located near the road's midpoint, it bears the name of Robert Lee ("Muley Bob") Doughton, a native of nearby Sparta who chaired the U.S. House Ways and Means Committee for all of Franklin D. Roosevelt's presidency and most of Harry Truman's. Doughton Park was originally named "The Bluffs"(for Bluff Mountain, its principal geographic feature). In 1951 it was renamed, at Doughton's friends' behest. Muley Bob was a parkway champion. He kept farmer's hours in Washington (in bed by 7 p.m., and at his office by 6 a.m.), wore size 15 shoes and ate apples with every meal. A wily politician, he rammed through legislation that placed the parkway permanently under the US Department of the Interior, insuring that it never became just another secondary road. The first of three parkway lodges was built at Doughton Park. The park has the parkway's most extensive trail system (30 miles), two campgrounds, picnic areas and a coffee shop. Works Progress Administration crews built the park's wood rail fences and restored Brinegar Cabin (MP 238.5), one of its cultural sites, in 1941-42. Unlike the remote Caudill Cabin, the homestead of Martin and Caroline Brinegar is easily accessible to visitors. Though a barn was removed to make way for the parkway, other buildings on the Brinegar farmstead—a granary, outhouse, springhouse and the cabin itself—remain in their original locations. You can get a bird's eye glimpse of the Caudill Cabin—in a tiny clearing in Basin Cove—from Wildcat Rocks overlook (MP 241.1), where there's also a plaque honoring Bob Doughton.

The Cascades at E.B. Jeffress Park, milepost 272

JEFFRESS PARK (MP 271.9-274.2)

The necessary land was never acquired for the major development once planned for Tompkins Knob, as this 1008-acre day-use area was originally known. E.B. Jeffress, for whom the park was renamed in 1964, chaired the NC Highway Commission in the 1930s and fought successfully to keep the parkway from becoming a toll road. The park's three principal features are the Cascades, a waterfall visible along a 0.6-mile trail; a picnic area; and a cluster of historic structures: Cool Springs Baptist Church, the Jesse Brown Cabin and a springhouse. Cabin and church have been relocated and reconstructed. In 1905, the cabin's owner moved it to its current location (to be closer to a spring). The church—in use as a barn when the parkway acquired it in the 1930s—was moved to the same clearing, within sight of the parkway, when the parkway reconstructed it. The unchinked saddle-notched log springhouse stands in the woods below the cabin.

CONE MANOR (MP 292.7-295)

Bertha Cone, widow of "Denim King" Moses H. Cone, didn't like the idea of the parkway coming through her 3512-acre estate and tried to pull strings to get the pleasure road rerouted. Parkway designers didn't give in; instead they delayed construction though that area until after Mrs. Cone died (1947). Their patience paid off. In 1950, the Cone heirs deeded the estate to the National Park Service. The estate is an anomaly: most parkway cultural sites interpret life of native highlanders, not of wealthy flatlanders who summered in the Blue Ridge. Cone Park's two principal draws are Flat Top Manor, the Cones' 23-room Beaux Arts mansion, and 25 miles of carriage trails that wind through fields and forest. The Southern Highland Handicraft Guild has operated the manor house as a craft and information center since 1951. (Be sure to stop and take in the view from a rocker on its long front porch.) The carriage trails are popular for hiking and horseback riding. One leads past the Cones' graves to an observation tower atop Flat Top Mountain; others explore woodlands and circle the estate's artificial lakes. The Cones assembled the estate at the end of the 19th century

Moses Cone Estate, milepost 293

from land they bought from subsistence farmers, whom they invited to stay on as employees, because they wanted the estate—with its orchards, crops, dairy operation and school—to be self sufficient. When the parkway acquired the estate a half century later, it removed all but five of its 57 buildings and evicted its tenants. Parts of the estate are under agricultural lease (see Design p. 85 for discussion).

PRICE PARK (MP 295-298.6)

Adjacent to Cone Manor is 4264-acre Price Park. It's named for Jefferson Standard Life Insurance

Sugar maple at Price Lake, milepost 297

president and CEO Julian Price, who acquired the land for a mountain retreat for company employees. After he died in an auto accident in 1946, the company and Price's children donated the land to the parkway, which developed it for outdoor recreation. Forty-seven-acre Price Lake is the parkway's largest water feature; Price Park campground is also the parkway's largest. The park's three hiking trails include an easy 2.3-mile level stroll around the lake, which is stocked with trout for anglers, and used for non-motorized boating. The park also includes a large picnic area and a comfort station.

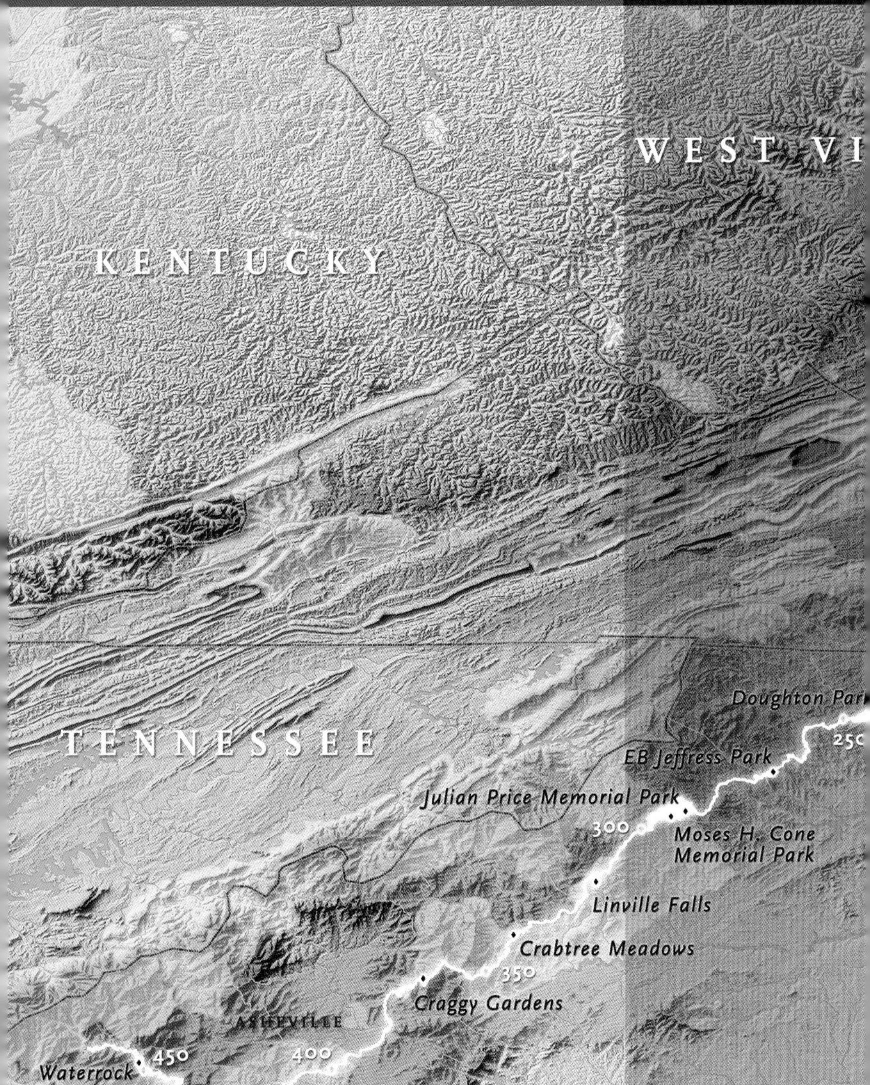
WEST VI
KENTUCKY
TENNESSEE
Doughton Par
250
EB Jeffress Park
Julian Price Memorial Park
300
Moses H. Cone
Memorial Park
Linville Falls
Crabtree Meadows
350
Craggy Gardens
ASHEVILLE
450
400
Waterrock
Knob
Mt. Pisgah

MILEPOST

305-469

Pisga

THE MO

Humpback Rocks

Whetstone Ridge

50

Otter Creek

James River

100

Peaks of Otter

LYNCHBURG

ROANOKE

Roanoke Mountain

VIRGINIA

150

Smart View

Rocky Knob

Mabry Mill

200

DANVILLE

Cumberland Knob

VIRGINIA

WINSTON-
SALEM

GREENSBORO

NORTH CAROLINA

RALEIGH

CHARLOTTE

eacon Heights to Oconaluftee River ...

UNTAINS

Twin Tunnels, milepost 345

THE MOUNTAINS: 305-469
Pisgah: Beacon Heights to Oconaluftee River

Visitor Centers

Linville Falls	316.4
Museum of North Carolina Minerals (open year round)	331.0
Craggy Gardens	364.5
Folk Art Center (open year round)	382.0
Waterrock Knob	451.2

Campgrounds

Linville Falls (50 tent, 20 RV)	316.4
Crabtree Meadows (71 tent, 22 RV)	339.5
Mt. Pisgah (70 tent, 70 RV)	408.8
Balsam Mountain Campground (46 sites, can accommodate RVs up to 30' long *off Heintooga Spur Road, is 8.4 miles off the parkway in Great Smoky Mountains National Park)*	458.2

Picnic Areas

Linville Falls	316.5
Crabtree Meadows	339.5
Craggy Gardens	367.6
Mt. Pisgah	407.8
Heintooga Ridge *(8.9 miles off the parkway on a spur road, in Great Smoky Mountains National Park)*	458.2

Lodging/Restaurants

Crabtree Meadows (restaurant only)	339.5
Mt. Pisgah Inn	408.6

Elevation Extremes

High point: **6053** ft. at Richland Balsam highest point on the parkway.	431.4
Low point: **2020** ft. at the Oconaluftee River	469.0

near the parkway's southern terminus. Other low points occur at other river crossings: 2040' at the Swannanoa River, MP 383.6; 2133' where the parkway crosses the French Broad, MP 393, on a high bridge *(the river itself is at 2000 feet);* and 3257' at the Linville River, MP 316.5. The road also dips at gaps: 2819' at Gillespie Gap, MP 330.9. West of Asheville, the most significant descent is to Balsam Gap, MP 443, elevation 3370', a drop of nearly 2700 feet in less than 12 miles from Richland Balsam.

Remains of a spring thunderstorm, milepost 349

The Mountains section begins at Beacon Heights, south of the Linn Cove Viaduct, and ends, where the parkway ends, at Great Smoky Mountains National Park. Its first 40 miles—past Linville Falls, Chestoa View, Little Switzerland and Crabtree Meadows—feel like a continuation of the Highlands. Elevations remain between 3000-4000 feet as the parkway negotiates a succession of forested areas and clearings, with occasional panoramic views into the piedmont to the east and mountain valleys to the west.

Serious climbing begins at Buck Creek Gap (MP 344.1). Past the spur road to Mt. Mitchell's summit, the parkway reaches its highest point north of Asheville—5676′—at MP 358.5. For nearly 10 miles between Mitchell and Craggy Gardens the roadway levels out. Surrounded by shrubby heath balds and boreal spruce/fir forests, the parkway enters a new realm—one it's soon to lose (but only temporarily) on its descent into and long traverse of the French Broad

River's valley floor. Once across the river, it ascends the Pisgah Ledge. Climbing, the parkway tunnels through rock fortresses, and emerges again into light. It switches from one side of the ridge to the other, with long views to the left and right into forested valleys, across ridge after ridge.

For the 35 miles past Pisgah, the views are all tremendous. For awhile, Looking Glass Rock, with its bare stone face and topknot of trees, draws the eye at every east-facing overlook and vista. Then it disappears—is forgotten—as the road sails across the ridgetop mile after amazing mile. Space here is on a different order of magnitude; there's nothing but mountains, as far as the eye can see—mountains and limitless skies. At Richland Balsam the parkway reaches its ultimate elevation: 6053'. Soon afterward it nosedives into Balsam Gap, then recovers to sail up again to Waterrock Knob. In its final miles it parachutes slowly into the Qualla Boundary—drifting toward the Smokies and the home of the Cherokee.

White trillium

Highlights

The Museum of NC Minerals (MP 331), interprets Blue Ridge geology and the importance of the Spruce Pine Mining District. The museum, open year round, was expanded and updated in 2003.

All but one of the parkway's 26 tunnels occurs in this section—testimony to its ruggedness.

At Ridge Junction (MP 355.3), a 5-mile spur road

Blue Ridge Mountains

leads to Mt. Mitchell State Park, and 6684 ft. Mt. Mitchell, highest peak in eastern America. It is here that the parkway abandons the Blue Ridge to cross the Blacks, Craggies, Balsams and Plott Balsams in its final 114 miles.

The Folk Art Center (MP 382.1), open year round, houses a museum, as well as exhibition and sales space for the Southern Highland Handicraft Guild's 700+ members.

Tanasee Bald (MP 423.7) is the southernmost point on the parkway. Hereafter the motor road trends NW to connect to Great Smoky Mountains National Park. A parkway extension into Georgia—long contemplated but finally abandoned—would have begun here.

Views

The predominance of panoramic views of multiple forested ridges returns in a big way in the parkway's final 150 miles. Pisgah district is dominated by big mountains—views of and from them. Occasional up-close valley scenes serve as only minor distractions from the chorus of "Oh, wow!" down-and-distant views of arresting focal features like Looking Glass Rock, unspoiled forests, and ridges stacked one upon another to the far horizon.

Construction history

Only six of the Pisgah District's 16 sections were completed by 1942. These included nearly 55 miles from the beginning of the district to Balsam Gap (MP 359.8) between Mt. Mitchell and Craggy Gardens, and a single 9.5-mile stretch west of Asheville—from US 19 (MP 455.7) to Big Witch Gap (MP 461.6). The remaining 99 miles were completed in the 1950s and 1960s. The last Pisgah District section to be built was from Swannanoa to the French Broad River (MP 383.6-393.5). Construction in the district was delayed for several reasons: the difficulty of the terrain; expense involved in building bridges and tunnels; and negotiations with the Eastern Band of the Cherokee about the parkway's route through the Indian reservation.

Recreational areas

Linville Falls (mp 316.4-316.6)

Had you visited Linville Falls 80 years ago, you'd have paid 10 cents for the privilege. That's what entrepreneur Fritz Hossfeld charged tourists after he bought the falls in 1919 from the Morganton Land and Improvement Company, which had planned to develop the area but fell on financial hard times. By 1938, Parkway planners were eyeing the falls, but lacked the money to acquire them. Finally, former park service director Horace Albright interested his friend John D. Rockefeller Jr., in buying them for the park service. Initially, Rockefeller wanted only to match funds from other sources, but in 1951 he agreed to foot the entire $100,000 bill for the falls and surrounding 1100 acres. Hiking trails to pedestrian overlooks above and below the falls were built before the 1.5-mile connecting road to the parkway was constructed. The recreation area includes a picnic area, campground, visitor center and a network of trails, one of which—the Linville

Table Rock in Linville Gorge, milepost 316

Linville Falls, milepost 316

Falls (Erwins View) Trail—was named a National Recreational Trail in 1981. The trail offers views not only of the falls, but into Linville Gorge, a 1500-foot deep chasm (deepest in Eastern America), which became the first designated wilderness area in the East in 1951.

CRABTREE MEADOWS (MP 339.5-340.4)

Identified early on as a desirable location for a campground, Crabtree Meadows offers a picnic area, campsites, snack and souvenir shop, restrooms and a 2.6 mile loop trail to a 60' waterfall. Parkway construction through the area began in 1937, preceding development of the recreation area by several years. The area had been logged extensively (part of the trail to the falls follows an old logging railway grade) and logging continued into the 1930s. Loggers and their families lived in the meadows area, in a community with a gristmill, commissary, smithy and a church that doubled as a school. In 1941 the US Forest Service transferred part of its holdings in the area to the parkway. Conscientious objectors, housed in an old Civilian Conservation Corps (CCC) camp below Buck Creek Gap, built trails and the original picnic area (where the campground is today). The campground was added after the parkway acquired more USFS land. The current picnic area opened in 1960, when the original picnic grounds was converted into another camping loop.

CRAGGY GARDENS (MP 363.4-369.6)

The heath balds of the Great Craggies, which glow pink when the Catawba rhododendron bloom, were a popular 19th century tourist attraction. That changed in 1920, with the establishment of the Asheville and

Craggy Pinnacle Trail, milepost 364

Woodfin watersheds. Thereafter, grazing animals, picnickers and campers were warned away from the cloud-wreathed Craggies. The Asheville Watershed Authority even dynamited a natural rock shelter to prevent campers from using it. Asheville civic organizations struck back in the 1930s; they arranged construction by the CCC of the "Scenic Elk Mountain Highway" (now NC 694) up the eastern slope of the Craggies, with a connecting trail to Craggy Pinnacle and Dome. In 1938, CCC boys built a hexagonal trail shelter and a picnic shelter in the Craggies, part of a US Forest Service effort to develop part of the Pisgah National Forest. Eventually, the Forest Service ceded 700 acres (including both shelters) to the parkway, which had altered its original route to include the mountain range's spectacular floral displays and wild scenery. This high elevation (5497') recreational area, with its picnic grounds, parking overlooks, visitor center and comfort station is especially popular in June, when the rhododendron bloom, in summer when the blueberries ripen, and during fall foliage season. Craggy Gardens' trail network connects to USFS trails and the NC Mountains-to-Sea Trail.

Mt. Pisgah (mp 407.6-408.7)
Graveyard Fields (mp 418.8)
Devil's Courthouse (mp 422.4)
Richland Balsam (mp 431.4)

George Vanderbilt built himself a massive hunting lodge at Buck Springs in 1898, on the shoulders of a mountain the Cherokee called Elseetoss and white settlers renamed Pisgah (for the place where Moses first glimpsed the Promised Land). In 1917, Vanderbilt's widow sold 80,248 acres, including Mt. Pisgah, to the US Forest Service. But it wasn't until mid-century that the parkway acquired holdings in the Pisgah area—including Vanderbilt's lodge. The parkway razed the lodge—and later the Pisgah National Forest Inn, established in 1919 by George Weston, Vanderbilt's former farm superintendent. Mt. Pisgah Inn fills its predecessor's niche. Parkway plans to develop major recreation areas south of Pisgah—at Graveyard Fields and Tanasee Bald (MP 423.7) never materialized. So Pisgah—with its inn, restaurant, campground, picnic area, restrooms and half-dozen hiking trails—remains the parkway's only multi-use developed area south of Asheville. Within 25 miles of it are Graveyard Fields, Devil's Courthouse and Richland Balsam. They're popular spots, thanks to their superior scenery. But they lack amenities beyond the hiking they offer (best at Graveyard Fields), and a single picnic table at Devil's Courthouse.

Waterrock Knob (mp 451.2)

A 24,000-acre protected area for the Plott Balsams—proposed by a park service location engineer in 1935—it isn't. But Waterrock Knob does provide the only visitor information center south of Mt. Pisgah. What you'll find, in addition to an information desk and restrooms, are peerless views of the Smokies to the west and the Great Balsams to the east—and a half-mile trail to the knob's 6300' summit. (The Waterrock itself is an exposed rock face to the southeast.) Waterrock Knob was once known as Amos Plott Balsam Mountain. It's one of several adjacent peaks that were named for individual members of the Plott family, descendents of a German immigrant who arrived on American shores in 1750 with a pack of hunting dogs. The Plotts who moved into this mountain fastness developed the dogs into a famous breed of bear hounds. A roadside plaque at an overlook on the short spur road to Waterrock Knob honors the contributions of highway engineer R. Getty Browning, who helped locate the parkway through North Carolina.

Coneflowers at Richland Balsam, milepost 431

DESIGN

Tye River Gap Bridge, 1941, milepost 27

EVERY ASPECT

OF THE PARKWAY DRIVING
EXPERIENCE WAS DESIGNED.
THE LANDSCAPE ARCHITECTS
WHO PLANNED THE PARKWAY
WANTED IT TO LIE LIGHTLY
ON THE LAND—TO FOLLOW
BLUE RIDGE TOPOGRAPHY
"AS THOUGH NATURE HAD
PUT IT THERE." THAT MEANT
MAKING THE ROAD BLEND
WITH ITS SURROUNDINGS
RATHER THAN STAND OUT
IN CONTRAST TO THEM.

BRIDGES, VIADUCTS AND TUNNELS

In places, parkway designers faced complexities
that required something more than hugging the
landscape. You'll find bridges, viaducts and tunnels
at these spots. Each solved a different problem.
Bridges carried the parkway over other roadways or
watercourses. Viaducts bridged dry ravines in steep
terrain, eliminating switchbacks, steep grades and
cutting and filling that would have created huge scars.
Tunnels were drilled where ridges were encountered
that ran perpendicular to the roadway's alignment.
In its 469 miles, the parkway crosses 170 bridges
and viaducts—and tunnels through 26 side ridges.

top: Fall colors along parkway
bottom: Linn Cove Viaduct, milepost 304

Little Switzerland Tunnel, milepost 334

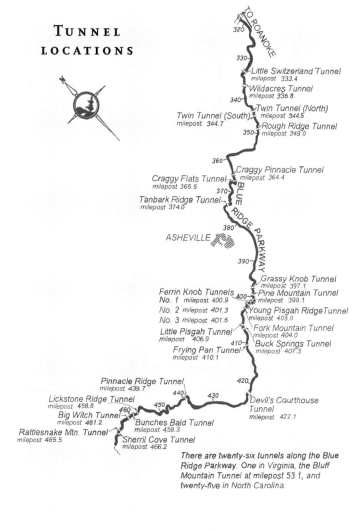

TUNNEL LOCATIONS

TO ROANOKE
320

330

Little Switzerland Tunnel
milepost 333.4

Wildacres Tunnel
milepost 336.8

340

Twin Tunnel (North)
milepost 344.5

Twin Tunnel (South)
milepost 344.7

Rough Ridge Tunnel
350
milepost 349.0

360

Craggy Pinnacle Tunnel
milepost 364.4

Craggy Flats Tunnel
milepost 365.5

370

Tanbark Ridge Tunnel
milepost 374.0

BLUE RIDGE PARKWAY

380

ASHEVILLE

390

Grassy Knob Tunnel
milepost 397.1

Ferrin Knob Tunnels
No. 1 milepost 400.9   400   Pine Mountain Tunnel
No. 2 milepost 401.3   milepost 399.1
No. 3 milepost 401.5

Young Pisgah Ridge Tunnel
milepost 403.0

Little Pisgah Tunnel
milepost 406.9

Fork Mountain Tunnel
milepost 404.0

Buck Springs Tunnel
410
milepost 407.3

Frying Pan Tunnel
milepost 410.1

420

Pinnacle Ridge Tunnel
milepost 439.7

440   430

Lickstone Ridge Tunnel
milepost 458.8   450

Devil's Courthouse
Tunnel
milepost 422.1

460

Big Witch Tunnel
milepost 461.2

Bunches Bald Tunnel
milepost 459.3

Rattlesnake Mtn. Tunnel
milepost 465.5

Sherril Cove Tunnel
milepost 466.2

There are twenty-six tunnels along the Blue Ridge Parkway. One in Virginia, the Bluff Mountain Tunnel at milepost 53.1, and twenty-five in North Carolina.

Selected portions from: Historic American Engineering Record NC-42, National Park Service, delineated by Lia M. Dikigoropoulou, 1997.

BY THE SIDE OF THE ROAD

Mileposts

Parkway mileposts are located on the roadway's grassy verge. First installed in 1947, the posts were designed for maximum long-distance visibility. They're three-sided, with the number of miles from the northern terminus incised on the two sides angled toward the road.

Signs

Parkway signs range from rustic wood to modern reflectorized metal and serve regulatory, informational and interpretive functions. Most regulatory signs—those providing safety and access information—resemble or are identical to those on ordinary highways. More distinctive are parkway informational signs: entrance signs installed at major

Mount Mitchell Overlook, milepost 350

parkway access points; trail system signs at places like Doughton Park and Rocky Knob. But the signs unique to the parkway are the routed wood "story signs" that recount local legends and historical lore. The parkway began installing these signs in 1941-42. They're called "gunboard" signs because their identifying marker is a pioneer squirrel rifle and powder horn. In 1959, someone noticed that the rifle lacked a ramrod. The design was subsequently corrected and future gunboard signs incorporated this feature.

The parkway's logo, with its curve of road slicing between a silhouetted Virginia pine and a mountain peak, appears on many signs. Its "parkway blue" pigment simulates the deep blue of the mountains in late evening. The driftwood gray background color was chosen to harmonize with the weathered wood of unpainted cabins and barns along the road. Entrance signs and most of the access signs posted near highway/parkway interchanges sport the parkway logo. A few of the latter, however, date from an earlier era and use the National Park arrowhead logo mounted on a slanting post.

Overlook signs—horizontal gray rectangles with routed white lettering—provide overlook names and parkway elevations. (Some also include the elevation of the view's focal

Selected portions from: Historic American Engineering Record NC-42, National Park Service, delineated by Cheria Yost and Matt Stormont, 1997:

MILE POST MARKER, 1947
(Photo 1953)

GUN BOARD, 1941

ENTRY SIGN, 1948

CURRENT ENTRY SIGN, from 1949

1960s ACCESS SIGN

MODERN ACCESS SIGN

point.) Brown and white metal "overlook ahead" signs indicate which side of the road the upcoming overlook is on—but subtly—by flipping the design to locate the pullout on the proper side of the roadway. (Note: the longest horizontal branch on the pine tree on the sign points to the side of the road the overlook is on.) Other brown and white signs announce approaches to recreational areas.

BUILDINGS

Ninety of the parkway's 336 buildings are classified as historic structures. Most serve as visual roadside features, evoking a sense of the isolation of Blue Ridge homesteads. Kelly springhouse (MP 150.8) and Sheets cabin (MP 252.3) are examples. Though these structures look as if they were built where they stand, many were moved from original sites to roadside locations. (Exceptions are Mabry Mill (MP 176.2), Puckett Cabin (MP 189.9) and Brinegar Cabin (MP 238.5) at Doughton Park.) An easily accessible complex of "pioneer" structures is assembled at the

Mabry Mill, milepost 176

Polly Woods Ordinary at Peaks of Otter, milepost 86

Farm Museum at Humpback Rocks. (The chicken house, root cellar and cowshed/corn crib all came from the John C. Clark Farm at MP 36.4, while the log cabin came from the Hamilton farm at MP 51.7.) Other historic structures—Polly Wood's Ordinary and the Johnson Farm at Peaks of Otter, the Caudill Cabin at Doughton Park and buildings on the Cone Estate— aren't visible from the roadway.

Also of historic interest are trail and picnic shelters erected in the 1930s and 1940s, when the parkway was being built, including those at Rocky Knob, Cumberland Knob, Doughton Park and Craggy Gardens. Noteworthy too are early concession buildings: the coffee shop at Otter Creek; camp store at Peaks of Otter; and the coffee shop and lodge at Doughton Park. These parkway-built structures were constructed in styles that echoed the architectural styles of the region, with board-and-batten, clapboard and masonry walls and shake roofs. (The "wood" shakes on the parkway buildings are actually concrete, made to resemble wood.)

More modern parkway buildings—the lodges at Peaks of Otter and Mt. Pisgah, the Folk Art Center, parkway headquarters, and the buildings at the Blue Ridge Music Center—also borrow their look from historic Blue Ridge structures to harmonize with older parkway buildings.

ROADSIDE SETTINGS AND VIEWS

Most roads and highways are designed to get you from Point A to Point B as quickly and safely as possible. The parkway, however, is concerned with your experience of getting from Point A to Point B. That experience is governed by the road's immediate surroundings (its setting) and what you see beyond (its views). Parkway landscape architects consciously created the road's setting. They had to, not only because parkway construction left scars, but because the surrounding countryside had been badly degraded by chestnut blight and by erosion caused by massive timber-cutting and over-farming.

Dogwood in Pisgah National Forest

Sunrise at Licklog Ridge Overlook, milepost 349

To create the parkway experience, its designers worked cinematically. Scene by scene, they composed a contrived landscape within a natural setting. To help the two blend, they planted only native species—indigenous plants reintroduced into habitats in which they would naturally occur. (In this they were ahead of their time—ahead even of ours.) Where they belonged, they planted rhododendron, flame azalea, mountain laurel, dogwood—understory shrubs and small trees whose dramatic blooms briefly light up the woods like fireworks, then fade from view.

But their greatest cinematic tool was manipulating the forest edge. They pulled it back from the road to broaden the view, then let it move back in. At the end of a long green tunnel, they pulled it back again, like a stage curtain, to expose a farm scene or a cabin in a clearing. In woodlands, they carved out grass, wild-flower, shrub and woods bays (small clearings). They planted specimen trees. They did all this to create variety and visual excitement—to stimulate travelers into wondering what lay around the next curve.

OVERLOOKS AND VISTA CUTS

Think of an overlook as an engraved invitation. The parkway issues more than 250 of them in 469 miles. These are places to stop and feast your eyes on beyond-the-park scenery. Depending on topography, overlooks can be nothing more than a paved pullover separated from the roadway by a painted white line. Others are more generously proportioned, with grassy—even wooded—islands between parking areas and motor road. Still others lead to dead-in parking areas (if you're driving an RV, watch for signs at entries and avoid these) or to loops that offer balcony views into patchwork valleys of farm and forest, or vast panoramas of multiple ridges.

Though there are overlooks in every district, more are concentrated in the Ridge and Pisgah districts. (The Plateau district—where much of the time you're driving through, rather than above, the scenery—has fewest.) Though most do, not all overlooks involve distant views. Some, like those along Otter Creek, provide intimate glimpses into woodlands. Views at some overlooks have been lost. Sometimes this is intentional—to screen out encroaching development.

Chestoa View, milepost 321

Mountain laurel at Green Knob Overlook, milepost 350

In other places, where trees blocking views are growing on non-parkway land, it's not.

There can be such a thing as too much scenery, "just as there can be too much ice cream or too much Beethoven," said an engineer who helped select the parkway route. To avoid a "seen-one-seem-'em-all" feeling, parkway designers treated overlook views in a variety of ways. At some, they cleared underbrush and trees' lower limbs to create a "canopy" or filtered view, where distant scenes are observed between the trunks of trees. At others, they cleared long swatches of vegetation to reveal breath-taking panoramas. At still others, they pulled the stage curtain only partway back, framing a view with nearby trees.

In addition to overlooks, there are numerous "vista clearings" along the motor road. There's no stopping place at these. Like windows in a winding hallway you must keep moving through, they build anticipation, enticing you to accept the next engraved invitation when it arrives.

In recent years, parkway staff has catalogued every

point along the motor road where you can see beyond the park boundary—1254 "view areas" in 469 miles. They've conducted surveys and identified 11 different "view types" which fall into four basic categories: views from the ridge into inhabited valleys; views of single or multiple forested ridges; rural farm views; and views that feature focal points like Stone Mountain, Looking Glass Rock, or the reservoir in the Asheville watershed. The number one choice of visitors, surveys revealed, are views that include water features. Think about it. What's your favorite kind of view?

Agricultural leases and scenic easements

Agricultural leases and scenic easements are two techniques the parkway uses to preserve views. The first involves land that the parkway owns; the second provides a way to control what happens on privately owned land visible from the motor road. The agricultural lease program was launched soon after the parkway began acquiring right-of-way through rural farmland. It was initiated because designers wanted to bring the farm scene up to the edge of the road. To do this, they leased farmland back to its former owners (or other farmers) for a nominal fee. But the leases came with strings attached. Because much of the land was badly eroded and worn out from over-farming, the parkway hired an agronomist who drew up conservation plans that required good farming practices—crop rotation, contour plowing, fertilization, cover cropping—as conditions for obtaining or renewing leases.

The parkway's agricultural lease program is one of its great—and continuing—successes. There are about 400 agricultural leases along the parkway today, most of them in the Plateau and Highlands districts. Many are held by descendents of the families who once owned the land. The program's benefits proved far-reaching and helped change farming practices—not only on parkway land, but in the surrounding countryside. Farmers saw their productivity rise on leased land and applied what they learned to their own acreage. Neighboring farmers noticed too, and adopted similar practices.

Though the leases continue, what's raised on them has changed dramatically in the last half century. Once plentiful row crops—potatoes, pumpkins, cabbages and squash—have all but disappeared. Today, row crops account for only 5 percent of leased land; the remainder is about equally divided between hay and pasturage. Another change—though you won't be able to see it—is that some leases are now being written to take wildlife conservation into account. (For instance, a lessee might be required to delay haying of some fields to give grassland bird species, which are declining, a chance to fledge their young.) Leased land is also being surveyed to locate rare, threatened and endangered plant and animal species.

Scenic easements allow the parkway to preserve views without having to own land outright. When a landowner sells or donates a scenic easement on part or all of his property, he agrees to deed restrictions that forever govern the way the land can be used. The parkway currently holds, monitors and manages more than 200 scenic easements. Both scenic easements and agricultural leases help blur the boundary between parkway and private land, and help foster the illusion that the park stretches from horizon to horizon.

RECREATIONAL AREAS

The parkway was designed to be a self-contained experience—a recreational destination for travelers looking to "drive awhile, stop awhile" as they moved along it at a leisurely pace. The road was engineered to be driven at about 45 mph, and designers wanted travelers to be able to "withdraw from the traffic" at frequent intervals to enjoy other forms of recreation. Initial plans called for major developed areas—with food, lodgings, campgrounds, gas stations, hiking and other recreational opportunities—roughly every 60 miles, with smaller "day-use" areas in between.

Parkway planners anticipated that visitors would stay on the parkway, once they reached it, partly because many neighboring communities were ill prepared to meet travelers' needs in the 1930s. Because the first

Craggy Pinnacle Tunnel, milepost 364

parkway segments were built in areas with the fewest topographic challenges—nearly all of the parkway through the high mountains south of Asheville was built after 1950—the intended pattern for recreational areas is easiest to see in the Ridge, Plateau and Highlands districts.

Planners looked for potential recreational areas when they were laying out the parkway route. As they traveled along, designer Stan Abbott said, "favorite places came into our thinking, and we might say to ourselves or out loud, 'We ought to control this,' or 'a gem.' Then we were guided, too, by a sense of need for rhythm or pattern—or a jewel on a string of beads occurring every so often, so there was a comprehensive plan, but not a rigid one." Large recreational areas required several thousand acres be acquired; smaller ones several hundred. They were to be "parks within a parkway."

RIDGE, MIDSLOPE, VALLEY, PLATEAU

Where are we now? What the mileposts don't tell you ...

You always know where you are on the parkway— at least in terms of your distance from its northern terminus. But another orienting factor affects your experience more than your distance from Rockfish Gap: where the particular section of road you're traveling on is located in relation to the surrounding landscape.

There are four possibilities. You're either on a ridge, the midslope (between a ridge and a gap), a plateau or in a valley. (You can be—and often are—on the ridge, even when you're outside the Ridge district, and there are plateau sections outside Plateau Country.) Each of these "landscape units" or "zones" can be characterized by its landform, vegetation and land use. Designers consciously moved the motor road from one zone to another to create variety in the visitor's experience.

Why does it matter whether you're on the ridge or plateau? For one thing, it governs what you see—and the way the road acts. On the ridge (which includes places where the road runs immediately below the actual ridgeline), the parkway tends to be relatively level. Your views are down and distant (of faraway objects below you), and the land is typically forested (though some is open). A disconnection between you and what you're looking at adds a sense of drama to ridge views. The parkway travels on the ridge about 29% of the time.

View near Richland Balsam, milepost 430

More than a third of the parkway (35%) is on the midslope. If you're on a prolonged climb or descent and the road is benched into the side of the mountain, you're probably on midslope. Most midslope is forested. Views are similar to ridge views—down and distant—though there's a sense you've dropped off (or haven't quite reached) your mountaintop perch. Most parkway overlooks are concentrated on the ridge and midslope.

When you're traveling in a valley, you have a sense of being enclosed, either by vegetation or by the topography (land form). Views are up close and personal—of what's immediately around you—so you feel like a part of the landscape you're moving

Bear Den Overlook, milepost 323

through. The road is relatively flat. The parkway
traverses valleys 17% of the time.

On a plateau (19% of parkway miles), views are similar
to those in a valley. There's a sense of enclosure, but
it comes more from vegetation than topography. You
feel as though you can see farther, when you're on
a plateau, than you can in a valley. The land is often
gently rolling.

Can you tell which landscape unit you're traveling
through? Use the clues we've listed and see if you
can figure out.

Farming along the parkway, 1946

FEATURES

CLIMATE, SEASONS, WEATHER

Drive the parkway in mid-summer and, other than temperature, you may not notice much difference between Apple Orchard Mountain and the James River Valley. Wildflowers stud roadsides; trees are a deep summer green. But if you make this trip as April melts into May, you'll feel as though you've engaged in a species of time travel. Trees in the valley are fully leafed out. Yet 15 miles away on the mountaintop, only the pink-tinged blooms of the serviceberry (locally known as "sarvis") hint that winter's stranglehold is about to be broken.

Step out at a parkway overlook in the spring or fall, and you may find yourself standing in one season, looking into another. Vast emerald seas engulf valleys in spring, rising like tides to overwhelm the high peaks. A few months later, fall's flames torch mountaintops first, then spread downhill like molten lava, inflaming the green world and leaving the high peaks bare.

Fraser magnolias near Three Knob Overlook, milepost 339

Grandfather Mountain from Yonahlossee Overlook, milepost 304

Elevation changes help explain these effects, though annual rainfall (40-85 inches, depending on location) and exposure also play roles. Generally, temperatures drop about three degrees for every 1000-foot rise in elevation—and parkway elevations vary by nearly 5500 feet, from 649' at the James River to 6053' at Richland Balsam. Frost-free days vary from about 100 days at highest parkway elevations to 200 at its lowest. That means the seasons proceed in a rush at high elevations—at a more leisurely pace lower down.

Temperature changes are often dramatic. In July, you can stand in wreathing mist at Craggy Gardens, goose bumps pinpricking your arms, then drive 15 miles to the Folk Art Center where the pavement radiates heat and there's not a sign of a cloud. Occasionally—and spectacularly—the effect is reversed. It's as though you're in a plane instead of a car, as you ascend from a fog-drowned valley into brilliant sunlight, with mountaintops floating like islands in an ocean of cloud.

The mountains make their own weather. That's

important for parkway travelers to keep in mind. If you're heading up for a day or two—even for an afternoon—don't forget a windbreaker. A sweatshirt. Sturdy shoes. Sunscreen. Snacks. An extra bottle of water. And allow yourself extra time, so that whatever you encounter can delight rather than frustrate you. Remember that there's no highway striping along the edge of the road. That can make driving in fog—and fog's no stranger to the mountains—a challenge. Use your low beams. Slow to a crawl.

Something else to remember: the parkway's nearly 500 miles follow mountains trending on a north/ south axis. That, combined with elevation changes and differences in exposure and rainfall, explains why you'll find habitats like those in Georgia, Newfoundland—and everywhere in between—on a motor road that's confined to just two states.

The parkway's "season" runs from May through October, though you're free to visit any time. Many parkway sections are closed during the winter due to ice and snow. Before you head for the parkway in winter, be sure to call the general information number (828-298-0398) to find out which sections are open. Remember, conditions can change daily. Be prepared.

FLORA

"When will the rhododendron bloom?" Parkway personnel field that question all the time. There's no good answer. For one thing, half a dozen different rhododendron species grow along the parkway— Catawba, Carolina and rosebay rhododendron, pinxter flower, and flame and pinkshell azalea. Pinxter flowers and Carolina rhododendron bloom as early as April in some locations; white-flowered rosebays as late as July. At low elevations, a species may bloom weeks before its buds begin to swell on the high peaks. The parkway publishes a bloom calendar (ask for it at visitor centers), but a better way to find out when to head to the Craggies, for instance, to see the rhododendron at their peak, is to call the general parkway information number (828-298-0398) and

Fire pink

Bloodroot

Turk's cap lilies

Larger blue flag iris

listen to the bloom report. It's updated weekly, and summarizes what's blooming where.

Though few people look for flowers in February, that's when the parkway's first plants bloom—pungent skunk cabbage and the lowly dandelion. They're followed by the year's first floral surge: spring ephemerals that carpet forest floors. There's a lull after that, before summer wildflowers kick in, though it's nearly impossible to travel the parkway between April and October and not find something blooming. Spring favorites include bloodroot, spring beauties, trillium,

Rosebay rhododendron, milepost 405

Dutchman's breeches, pink lady's slipper, squirrel corn, mayapple, dwarf crested iris and dozens more.

Summer's wildflower season is more extended than spring's and—like summer itself—more explosively colorful. The saturated yellows of coreopsis and primrose stand cheek by jowl to magenta phlox and fire pinks. Turk's cap lilies and Joe-Pye-weed tilt long stems toward the sun. Black-eyed Susans, coneflowers, wild sunflowers, goldenrods, cardinal flower, white snakeroot, purple asters and ironweed come on strong as their predecessors fade, carrying the wildflower display into the fall foliage season, when it's the maples, sourwoods and ashes that elicit oohs and aahs.

Not that the trees don't assert themselves earlier in the year. In early spring, redbuds and dogwoods spill down mountainsides and light up the forest edge. Magnolias' creamy candles glow. Pendant bloom clusters of Carolina silverbell and black locust, and the orange and yellow flowers of tulip poplars—not to mention the incandescent greens their leaves achieve immediately after bud break—make it worthwhile to check out the canopy as well as the ground. In mid-summer, look for sourwood's feathery flower sprays, splayed like long, pale fingers. The very last tree to bloom is witch hazel. Its faint yellow stars cling to bare branches when leaves crunch crisply underfoot.

Biodiversity is the parkway's middle name. Altogether 14 major vegetation types occur along it, including about 1250 species of vascular plants, 50 of them threatened or endangered. The parkway is home to nearly 100 species of trees—about the number in all of Europe—not to mention about 400 species of moss and nearly 2000 kinds of fungi.

FAUNA

You're not quite so assured of seeing them as you are of wildflowers, but the parkway is home to thousands of animal species (some of them admittedly very small). Best bets to see are mammals (54 species) and birds. Wild turkeys, reintroduced and making a great comeback, are a common sight, especially in the Highlands. Of the 4-footed creatures, you'll likely spot white-tailed deer (some shepherding fawns) and groundhogs (woodchucks), often standing bolt upright, as if counting passing cars. It's hard to believe that deer were so scarce here when the parkway was built that herds were imported from

Wild turkeys

Timber rattlesnake

Red salamander

Wisconsin for release in recreational areas like Doughton Park. Today, their exploding population threatens understory native plants, particularly in the Peaks of Otter area. They can also be a safety hazard for parkway drivers. Always be alert to the possibility of deer—often more than one—emerging from the forest edge to cross the parkway in front of your car.

Other commonly seen animals include squirrels (grays mostly, though red "boomers" may scold you at high elevations) and chipmunks high-tailing it across the road. Less frequently spotted are coyotes, gray or red foxes, skunks, river otters, raccoons, opossums and beavers. The parkway provides habitat for 12 species of bats, an assortment of moles, voles, mice, shrews, weasels and black bears. More than 50 fish species, and nearly as many kinds of amphibians and reptiles, are parkway residents. Of these, you're most likely to see snakes sunning on the pavement, or turtles stacked like muddy hubcaps on partially submerged logs. Ten frog species and dozens of kinds of salamanders inhabit parkway wetlands and woods.

On sunny summer days, butterflies drift like blown leaves across the motor road. Probably the most commonly-noticed is the tiger swallowtail—a large yellow and black butterfly whose caterpillars feed on tulip poplar leaves (one reason you see so many of them in forested areas). Open fields and meadows at recreational areas are good places to look for butterflies, so long as the sun is out. In September and October, watch for orange-and-black monarch butterflies migrating to overwintering sites in the mountains of central Mexico. Monarchs in large numbers sometimes cross the parkway at Cherry Cove overlook (MP 415.7), where there is an interpretive display on the monarch migration, and at an unnamed overlook (MP 352.4), just north of the spur road to Mt. Mitchell. But they're likely to be seen all along the Blue Ridge during migration, particularly after a cold front.

LANDMARKS

Because the ice sheets of glaciers never reached the Blue Ridge and Southern Appalachians, there is a notable lack of natural ponds and lakes in parkway country. And while the parkway passes a few historic millponds that predate its construction—Rakes and Little Glade millponds (at MP 162.4 and 230.1 respectively) are examples—most of the parkway's artificial impoundments date from the period of its construction. They include Otter Lake (MP 63.1), Abbott Lake (MP 85.9), the millpond at Mabry Mill

Price Lake, milepost 297

(MP 176.2) Sims Pond (MP 295.9) and Price Lake (MP 296.7). Originally, bathing beaches and changing houses were planned for lakes in recreational areas—and many more lakes were planned than were actually built—but these plans were later abandoned. Fishing—but no swimming—is allowed at parkway ponds and lakes.

The blasting and cutting that occurred during parkway construction created an inadvertent feature: the water that sluices or drips down exposed rock faces next to the road. These here-today-gone-tomorrow water features change with the seasons, even with time of day. In early morning in certain lights, wet rock looks metallic. In sunlight it sparkles. In winter, tremendous amounts of ice build up on some rock faces. Two outstanding spots for these water special effects are Ice Rock (MP 242) in Doughton Park, and rock faces between Craggy Gardens and the Folk Art Center (MP 364.5-382).

What the Blue Ridge lacks in natural lakes and ponds, it makes up for in moving water: streams, rivers and waterfalls. The two largest rivers it crosses are the James, which flows into the Atlantic Ocean, and the French Broad, whose waters end up in the Gulf of Mexico. (An overlook at MP 393.8 offers a good look at the latter river; an interpretive sign there details its historical significance.) The parkway crosses other rivers too: the Roanoke, Linville, Swannanoa and Oconaluftee. It traverses meandering streams: Otter Creek (between MP 57.6-63.1), and Chestnut and Pine creeks, on both sides of the NC/VA state line. From MP 139-355.3, the parkway roughly follows the Eastern Continental Divide. Between these mileposts, waters on its eastern flank are Atlantic bound; those on its west drain into the Mississippi and the Gulf of Mexico.

Topography explains the abundance of Blue Ridge waterfalls. Outstanding among them are Fallingwater Cascades (MP 83.1) at Peaks of Otter; the Cascades (MP 271.9) at Jeffress Park; Linville Falls (MP 316.4), Crabtree Falls (339.5), and two waterfalls on the Yellowstone Prong of the East Fork of the Pigeon River at Graveyard Fields (MP 418.8). Only one of these is visible from the roadway, but trails lead to them.

In addition, there are many off-parkway waterfalls worth a detour. Two of the closest are Crabtree Falls, VA, and Looking Glass Falls, NC. To reach the former, exit the parkway at Tye River Gap (MP 27.2), and take VA 56 east toward Montebello. The waterfall is five miles from the parkway; parking area is on the right. For Looking Glass Falls, exit the parkway at MP 411.8 (US 276), turn left toward Cradle of Forestry. The falls are about 10 miles from the parkway on the left and are visible from your car.

Crabtree Falls, Virginia, milepost 27

Looking Glass Rock, milepost 415

Parkway geologic points of interest include monoliths visible from the motor road—Pilot and Stone Mountain and Looking Glass Rock—and parkway rock formations like Humpback Rocks and Devil's Courthouse. Trails to the tops of the latter two offer panoramic views of the surrounding countryside.

Overlooks provide views of prominences whose shapes suggested their names: House, Terrapin and Doubletop mountains, Chimney and Table rocks. Descriptive names for many natural features are drawn from local flora: Chestnut Ridge, White Oak Flats, Hickory Spring, Cherry Cove—and fauna: Beaver Dam Gap, Bear Den, Wolf Mountain, Deer Lick Gap and Wildcat Rocks. Human inhabitants left their mark at Bobblet's Gap, Jenkins Ridge, Boone's Trace, Sweet Annie Hollow and Betsey's Rock Falls.

RIDE AWHILE, STOP AWHILE

Designed as a destination as well as means to get from here to there, the parkway's a multipurpose road. And while the number one reason visitors travel the parkway is for its scenery, there's much to do besides motoring along.

Enjoy a Picnic: Fourteen designated picnic areas provide tables, fireplaces, drinking water and comfort stations. Fires (including charcoal grills) are allowed only in designated picnic areas. But picnicking is also permitted elsewhere unless otherwise posted. So pick

Picnic area near Flat Rock Trail, milepost 308

a spot, pull off the road, and spread a blanket. (Tips for picnickers: pack a plastic tablecloth with flannel backing for parkway picnic tables. The flannel helps the cloth adhere to rough table surfaces and resists a breeze. Bring a sponge in a plastic bag to wipe the cloth clean before repacking. The night before you

Devil's Courthouse, milepost 422

plan to picnic, freeze an almost full gallon jug of water for your cooler. It will keep your food cool—better than bagged ice—and you can drink its melt.)

Camp Out: Four parkway campgrounds in Virginia and five in North Carolina offer travelers a variety of on-parkway facilities and activities. Camping elsewhere (except in a few back-country areas by permit only) is prohibited. A campground information sheet is available at visitor centers. See p. 124 for more on camping.

Take a Hike: More than 100 hiking trails offer another parkway perspective. They vary in length from easy leg-stretchers on nearly level ground to daylong expeditions covering miles of strenuous up and down. Lists of parkway trails, including their access points, length and level of difficulty, are available at visitor centers. In recreational areas, ask for trail maps.

About a dozen of the parkway's shorter trails are self-guided, with trailside plaques providing cultural or natural history. Find these in recreational areas at Humpback Rocks, James River, Peaks of Otter, Rocky Knob, E.B. Jeffress Park, Cone Manor; also at Roanoke River (MP 114.9), Flat Rock (MP 308.2), Craggy Gardens (MP 364.6) and Richland Balsam (MP 431). Many parkway impoundments are encircled by easy loops. Two short jaunts from overlooks that should not be skipped lead to superior views at Fox Hunter's Paradise (MP 218.6) and Chestoa View (MP 320.8).

Those who are in reasonable shape should climb to panoramic views at Humpback Rocks (MP 6), Sharp Top (MP 86), Craggy Pinnacle (MP 364.2), Mt. Pisgah (MP 407.6), Devil's Courthouse (MP 422.4) and Waterrock Knob (MP 451.2). (You can avoid most of the 1.6-mile uphill climb to Sharp Top's summit by taking a bus most of the way up; ride or hike back down.) The Lump's 0.3-mile trail at MP 264.4 is worth stopping for. A longer (but moderate) hike— 5.6 miles round-trip—takes you to a viewing tower atop Flat Top Mountain on the Cone Estate.

Everyone should sample Cone Park's 25-miles of carriage trails and the 13.5-mile Tanawha Trail that

Craggy Pinnacle Trail, milepost 364

parallels the parkway between Beacon Heights
and Price Park. (Numerous trailheads at parkway
overlooks between MP 298.6-304.4 offer access to
this beautifully constructed trail, with its arched
wooden bridges and stone stairways.) For the long-
distance hiker, the parkway offers some excellent
choices, among them the 10.8-mile loop trail around
Rock Castle Gorge and Doughton Park's 30-mile trail
network. And don't overlook the chance to hike parts
of the AT, North Carolina's Mountains-to-Sea Trail or
connecting Forest Service trails.

Wear appropriate footwear (hiking shoes or boots for all but the leg-stretchers); lock valuables in the trunk or take them with you; and carry drinking water and suitable clothing for sudden weather changes. Stay on established trails, including boardwalks, to avoid trampling fragile plant life. Do not climb over retaining walls.

Ride a Bike: The parkway's designers surely did not envision its future popularity with cyclists, who cite its superb engineering and scenery among its appeals. Parkway drivers should always be on the lookout for cyclists. Cyclists are required to wear helmets and high visibility clothing, to travel single file well to the right-hand side of the road, to use a front headlight in tunnels, and to exhibit reflectors. Cycling is limited to paved road surfaces and parking areas (no mountain or other bikes on trails or walkways). An information sheet on parkway cycling, available at visitor centers, lists regulations, safety suggestions and all major uphills (and elevations climbed) for cyclists traveling north or south.

Catch a Fish: In addition to the parkway's 13 artificial lakes and ponds, its acreage is drained by more than 100 miles of streams that provide habitat for dozens of native and stocked fish species. Fishing is permitted from half an hour before sunrise to half an hour after sundown. You must hold a valid state license from either Virginia or North Carolina and use single hook, artificial lures. Special regulations or closed waters for specific streams are clearly marked on those watercourses.

Watch Birds: The parkway's many habitats and constant elevation changes make it bird watcher's heaven. By providing convenient access to habitats that are normally difficult to reach, it attracts flocks of birders, especially during spring and fall migrations. More than 200 bird species use the parkway regularly, either to nest or to migrate. A measure of the parkway's importance to birds is that many Important Bird Areas (listed through an international effort to identify areas crucial to bird species) are clustered along it. Among the rarities that are found with fair regularity at specific parkway locations are red

Abbott Lake at Peaks of Otter, milepost 86

crossbills, saw-whet owls and cerulean warblers. High elevation spruce-fir forests provide habitat for red-breasted nuthatches, brown creepers, winter wrens, black-capped chickadees and ravens. Good spots for these are the trail to the top of Devil's Courthouse (MP 422.4) and Heintooga Spur Road (MP 458.2).

In the fall, hawk watchers congregate at Afton Inn at Rockfish Gap (MP 0), and at Harvey's Knob (MP 95.3), Mahogany Rock (MP 235) and Mills River Valley overlook (MP 404.5). They're looking for broad-winged hawks, peregrine falcons, ospreys, bald eagles and other raptors migrating from summer homes in the U.S. and Canada to wintering grounds as far away as South America. (Look for hawks also at other ridgetop sites like Rocky Knob and Doughton Park.) When warblers wearing their bright breeding plumage fly north in spring, birders head for "Warbler Road," a 13-mile network of forest service and county roads that begins near the northern end of Sunset Field Overlook (MP 78.4) on FSR 812 and drops to the James River.

Red-tailed hawk

Other good warbler (and birding) spots are Peaks of Otter (with breeding cerulean and Canada warblers), Rocky Knob/Rock Castle Gorge, Doughton Park, and the parkway between Mt. Mitchell and Asheville (MP 355.3-MP 382).

You probably wouldn't associate the parkway with waterfowl, but its ponds and lakes draw them. In March or April see loons, mergansers, teal and buffleheads on Cone Park's Trout and Bass lakes; in summer, wood ducks, geese and mallards. Great blue herons nest on a Bass Lake island. The park's 30 nesting pairs of a Southern Appalachian subspecies of Yellow-bellied sapsucker make it the best location anywhere to see them.

Bird checklists are available for specific sections, covering most of the parkway. Find them at visitor centers or on the parkway website (www.nps.gov/blri) by clicking the "Nature and Science" link.

Discover Handicrafts: A cultural heritage rich in handicrafts permeates the parkway and its environs. From Cherokee carvers, potters and basket-makers to blacksmiths who forged hand tools, woodworkers who fitted together chairs and sledges, and homemakers who turned cast-off clothing into patchwork quilts, mountain dwellers fashioned objects of great beauty and utility from materials at hand. The tradition continues today. Find handicrafts for sale at three parkway locations: Northwest Trading Post (MP 258.7), Moses Cone Manor House (MP 294) and the Folk Art Center (MP 382). Craft demonstrations are staged at the latter two, usually on weekends. Additionally, hundreds of craft studios and galleries are located within a few miles of the parkway. Ask at visitor centers about nearby locations for mountain crafts.

Tap a Toe to Mountain Music: The parkway's newest recreational area—the Blue Ridge Music Center (MP 213.3)—is designed to document and honor the importance of mountain music in the cultural history of the Blue Ridge and Southern Appalachians. In addition to the center, there are more than 150 venues within 30 miles of the parkway in which traditional music is regularly presented. Under traditional music's umbrella: gospel, bluegrass, country and western, old time, shape-note singing and many other musical forms. Venues vary from "hometown oprys" where local folks turn out to clog and buck dance to annual fiddler's conventions and radio shows. Jam sessions take place in barbershops, fire halls, and around tailgates at musical gatherings. On the parkway, weekend summer concerts are scheduled at the Blue Ridge Music Center. Music is also presented at Roanoke Mountain campground on Sunday evenings, at Mabry Mill on Sunday afternoons and at the Orchard at Altapass (MP 328.3) on Saturday and Sunday afternoons. See p. 42 for more about the Blue Ridge Music Center.

Learn a Little (or a Lot): Rangers and volunteers offer interpretive programs from June through October, mostly on weekends. Activities include campfire talks, music and history demonstrations, nature walks and slide presentations, and vary from area to area. Schedules are posted at visitor centers, campground entrances and parkway concessions. Young parkway visitors may participate in the parkway's "Junior Ranger Program" and earn a badge and certificate.

Other Outdoor Activities: Rock climbing, cross country skiing, hunter access to US Forest Service lands—even hang-gliding—are permitted in certain areas and under certain conditions, but should not be engaged in before obtaining pertinent information from visitor centers or rangers. If you're interested in any of these activities, inquire first.

Boone Fork along Tanawha Trail, milepost 300

PARKWAY PICKS

FIVE FAVORITE
FLOWER PATCHES,
PICNIC STOPS,
HIKING TRAILS,
BIRDING SPOTS,
FALL COLOR VIEWS,
OVERLOOKS AND
WATERFALLS ...

Parkway, prior to paving, just south
of Daniel Gap, 1936, milepost 262

Pink lady's slippers

FLOWERS

Otter Creek to Sunset Field Overlook: MP 57.6-78.4
Redbud, dogwood, pinxter flower show in April and
May; August brings summer wildflowers including
composites, and Joe-Pye-weed.

Rocky Knob to Mabry Mill: MP 167.1-176.2
Rhododendron varieties, flame azalea and
mouintain laurel bloom in May and June.

Chestoa View to Crabtree: MP 320.8-339.5
Spring wildflowers abound in April and May
including trillium, crested iris, and pink lady's slippers.

Craggy Gardens: MP 364.5
Visit in June for an annual Catawba rhododendron explosion.

Mt. Mitchell to Folk Art Center: MP 355.3-382
July and August signal the arrival of summer wildflowers
such as coneflowers, bee balm, coreopsis and Turk's cap lily.

Waterrock Knob, milepost 451

PICNICS

Raven's Roost: MP 10.7
Get a bird's eye view of Shenandoah Valley.

Abbott Lake: MP 85.9
Throw down a blanket along the lakeshore.

Crabtree Meadows: MP 339.5
Want to picnic, but didn't bring food?
Pick something up at the snack bar,
then cross the parkway to a table.

Waterrock Knob: MP 451.2
Set up a tailgate party in the parking lot and watch
the sun descend over the Great Smoky Mountains.

Heintooga: MP 458.2, then 8.9 miles on spur road
Enjoy a remote, magical spot for those
seeking a road less traveled.

Rock Castle Gorge Trail, milepost 167

HIKES

Sharp Top at Peaks of Otter: MP 85.9
A mountaintop worth visiting
—not only for the view.

Rock Castle Gorge Trail, Rocky Knob: MP 169
A 10.8-mile loop for experienced hikers;
gorge rim for stroll.

Carriage Trails at Moses Cone: MP 294
Everyone should sample Cone Park's
25-miles of carriage trails.

Plunge Basin, Linville Falls: MP 316.4
Hike through an old growth forest to
a bottom-up view of falls.

Mt. Pisgah: MP 407.6
Enjoy 360-degree views from
summit observation platform.

Barred owl

BIRDS

Rockfish Gap: MP 0
Visit September 15-30 to see migrating
broad-winged hawks. Other raptors can be seen
during months of September and October.

Warbler Road: begins near MP 78.4
Warblers can be seen mid-April to late May.

Moses Cone Park: MP 294
Warblers, Appalachian subspecies, Yellow-bellied Sapsucker,
and waterfowl can be seen throughout the year.

Craggy Gardens Visitor Center: MP 364.5
From late summer into fall, migrating thrushes, warblers,
grosbeaks can be seeen during early morning hours.

Black Balsam Road: MP 420.2 & **Devil's Courthouse**: MP 422.4
Summer is recommended for high elevation species
(Specialties: least and alder flycatchers at Black Balsam;
breeding peregrine falcons at Devil's Courthouse).

Linville Gorge, milepost 316

FALL COLORS

Peaks of Otter: MP 85.6
Take a stroll around Abbott Lake or enjoy
panoramic views from the heights of Sharp Top.

Mabry Mill: MP 176.2
Colors are usually nice around the mill,
but combine bluegrass music with the aroma
of baked apples and it will "feel like fall."

Grandfather Mountain: MP 305.1
Higher elevations of this magnificent mountain
usually loose their leaves quickly but lower areas
that the parkway passes through are spectacular.

Linville Gorge: MP 316.4
Autumn's canvas is everywhere you look.

Graveyard Fields: MP 418.8
Mountain ash makes this a particularly colorful destination.

Green Knob Overlook, milepost 350

OVERLOOKS

Twenty Minute Cliff: MP 19
When a summer day's last rays of sunlight shone
only on this cliff, farmers working in the valley below
knew they had twenty minutes remaining until sunset.

Chestoa View: MP 320.8
A short trail from the parking area leads to a panoramic vista
of North Cove and the upper reaches of Linville Gorge.

Green Knob Overlook: MP 350.4
Visit this overlook at different times of day and
in different seasons and you will truly appreciate the
dynamic nature of the Blue Ridge Parkway.

Mills River Valley Overlook: MP 404.5
Be sure to check out the views from both sides of the road.

Pounding Mill Overlook: MP 413.2
Catch a sunrise from this overlook and then head
right down the parkway for breakfast at Pisgah Inn.

Upper Falls at Graveyard Fields, milepost 419

WATERFALLS

Fallingwater Cascades: MP 83.1 at Peaks of Otter
Visit after periods of rain to see this low volume falls at its best.

The Cascades: MP 271.9 at E.B. Jeffress Park
Convenient overlooks are found at the top and middle
sections of this cascading waterfall. Visit in July
to see rosebay rhododendron blooming.

Linville Falls: MP 316.4
Is there a better location for watching
falling water anywhere in the Appalachians?

Looking Glass Falls: exit the parkway at MP 411.8
via US 276 and turn left toward Cradle of Forestry
An off-parkway waterfall worth the detour. The falls are about
10 miles from the parkway on the left, visible from your car.

Upper Falls at Graveyard Fields: MP 418.8
A 1.6 mile trail through Graveyard Fields leads hikers
upstream along Yellowstone Prong to the base of Upper Falls.

RESOURCES

Final section of parkway near Grandfather Mountain, 1976

Contact information

Blue Ridge Parkway: For general parkway information, including road and weather conditions, call **828-298-0398**, or visit the parkway website at: **www.nps.gov/blri**. To report accidents, emergencies or illegal activities, call: 1-800-PARKWATCH (**1-800-727-5928**). The number for parkway headquarters is **828-271-4779**.

VISITOR CENTERS: Parkway visitor centers are generally open from May through October. Most include information desks where you may pick up parkway information (bloom calendars, trail maps, camping and other recreational information, etc.) and sales areas offering parkway-related books and other educational products (field guides, etc.).

FOOD & LODGINGS: With the exception of Peaks of Otter, which is open year-round, parkway restaurants, coffee shops and lodgings are generally open from May through the end of October.

CAMPGROUNDS: Camping on the parkway is permitted only in designated camping areas. The parkway's 9 campgrounds are generally open from mid-May through November 1, though a few open in April. Winter camping (weather permitting) is occasionally available. Per night fee is subject to change. All campgrounds have both tent and RV sites—and sanitary dump stations (no water or electrical hookups). With the exception of Rocky Knob, campgrounds have at least one wheelchair-usable site. Campsites are available on a "first come, first served" basis, although reservations are accepted for some sites at Price Park and Linville Falls. (Reservations may be made online at reserveUSA.com or by calling **1-877-444 6777**.)

GAS: Although available at only one parkway location—Doughton Park (MP 241)—gas is available not far from the parkway on intersecting highways in Virginia and North Carolina.

Doughton Park, milepost 244

mile-post	destination	visitor center	dining	lodging	camp-ground	gift shop
	VIRGINIA					
5.8	Humpback Rocks	✔				✔
60.8	Otter Creek		✔		✔	✔
63.6	James River	✔				✔
85.9	Peaks of Otter	✔	✔	✔	✔	✔
115.0	Virginia's Explore Park	✔				✔
120.4	Roanoke Mountain				✔	
169.0	Rocky Knob	✔		✔	✔	✔
176.1	Mabry Mill		✔			✔
213.3	Blue Ridge Music Center	✔				✔
	NORTH CAROLINA					
217.5	Cumberland Knob	✔				✔
241.1	Doughton Park		✔	✔	✔	✔
258.6	Northwest Trading Post	✔				✔
294.0	Moses Cone Park	✔				✔
297.0	Julian Price Park				✔	
304.4	Linn Cove Viaduct	✔				✔
316.4	Linville Falls	✔			✔	✔
330.9	NC Minerals Museum	✔				✔
339.5	Crabtree Meadows		✔		✔	✔
364.6	Craggy Gardens	✔				✔
382.0	Folk Art Center	✔				✔
408.6	Pisgah Inn		✔	✔	✔	✔
451.2	Waterrock Knob	✔				✔

RELATED INFORMATION: National forests, nearby state and national parks and other facilities adjacent to the parkway, are listed below.

George Washington and Jefferson National Forest
540-265-5100; www.southernregion.fs.fed.us/gwj
Great Smoky Mountains National Park
865-436-1200; www.nps.gov/grsm
Mt. Mitchell State Park
828-675-4611
Nantahala and Pisgah National Forest
828-257-4200; www.cs.unca.edu/nfsnc
Shenandoah National Park
540-999-3500; www.nps.gov/shen

left to right: J. Scott Graham, Elizabeth C. Hunter, Gary W. Johnson and Kerry Scott Jenkins at Blue Ridge Parkway Headquarters in Asheville, North Carolina.

Crabtree Falls, North Carolina, milepost 339

Many Blue Ridge Parkway products by J. Scott Graham are available at visitor centers and at fine retailers throughout the region, or via the contact information below:

J. Scott Graham
316 Shawnee Road
Johnson City, TN 37604

www.jscottgraham.com
(423) 854-9435   Phone
(423) 854-9041   Fax

Contributors

J. Scott Graham has enjoyed the fascinating array of flora and fauna inherent to the Blue Ridge Mountains since lacing up his first pair of hiking boots at the age of fourteen. Having spent most of his life among these aged peaks, Graham still finds great pleasure in visiting and revisiting the scenery he calls home, to record the spectacular sights of this region on film. His dramatic images display a skillful observation of nature and passionate artistic vision that have earned him recognition as one of this country's premier landscape photographers. Over the years, Graham has utilized his images to become the most prolific publisher of products featuring the Blue Ridge Parkway, America's most popular national park site. He lives in Johnson City, Tennessee, with his wife Cathy, and their sons Chace and Jackson.

Kerry Scott Jenkins is a graphic designer who specializes in publication design and type design. He grew up in Spruce Pine, North Carolina (just off the Parkway at milepost 331), received a BFA from Western Carolina University, and his MFA in graphic design from East Tennessee State University. Most recently, Jenkins has founded Toye Books, and will publish his own children's books. He lives in Johnson City, Tennessee, with his wife Sherry and their kids, Matt and Kacey.

Elizabeth C. Hunter is a freelance writer who has been writing about the Blue Ridge Parkway for more than 20 years. As a newspaper reporter, she covered the parkway's 50th Anniversary Celebration and Conference in Boone and Cumberland Knob in 1985, and its 1987 Dedication at the Linn Cove Viaduct and Grandfather Mountain. She has written a series of articles on the parkway for *Blue Ridge Country Magazine,* for which she is a columnist and contributing editor, and wrote the essays for *Blue Ridge Parkway: America's Favorite Journey.*

Gary W. Johnson is Chief of the Blue Ridge Parkway's Resource Planning and Professional Services Division. A landscape architect, he began his National Park Service career with a three-year stint as a construction supervisor on the Blue Ridge Parkway, then spent 15 years as project manager/landscape architect and section chief at the National Park Service's Denver Service Center before returning to the parkway in 1994 to assume his current position. He has been instrumental in directing park staff in preserving the parkway's historic roadway features and buildings, conserving scenic views, protecting adjacent lands and establishing a system for scenery management.

MILEPOST INDEX